# TO KILL A MOCKINGBIRD

a full-length play
by
**Christopher Sergel**

based upon the novel
by
**Harper Lee**

**The Dramatic Publishing Company**
Woodstock, Illinois ● Wilton, Connecticut ● Melbourne, Australia

## *** NOTICE ***

Cover photo from the Mermaid Theatre production in London.
Starring Penny Gonshaw as Scout and Alan Dobie as Atticus.
Cover design: Susan Carle

# TO KILL A MOCKINGBIRD

A Play in Two Acts
For Eleven Men* and Six Women, Extras

## CHARACTERS

JEAN LOUIS FINCH (SCOUT) . . . . . . . . . . . a young girl
JEREMY FINCH (JEM) . . . . . . . . . . . . her older brother
ATTICUS FINCH . . . . . . . . . . . . . . . . . . . . . . .their father
CALPURNIA . . . . . . . . . . . . . . . . . . . . . . the housekeeper
MAUDIE ATKINSON ⎫
STEPHANIE CRAWFORD ⎪
MRS. DUBOSE ⎬ . . . . . . . . . . . neighbors
ARTHUR RADLEY (BOO) ⎭
CHARLES BAKER HARRIS (DILL) . . . . . a young boy
HECK TATE . . . . . . . . . . . . . . . . . . . . . . . . . . . . .the sheriff
JUDGE TAYLOR . . . . . . . . . . . . . . . . . . . . . . . . the judge
REVEREND SYKES . . . . . . . . . . . . . . . . . . . . . a minister
MAYELLA EWELL . . . . . . . . . . . . . . . . . . a young woman
BOB EWELL . . . . . . . . . . . . . . . . . . . . . . . . . . . . her father
WALTER CUNNINGHAM . . . . . . . . . . . . . . . . . a farmer
MR. GILMER . . . . . . . . . . . . . . . . . . . the public prosecutor
TOM ROBINSON . . . . . . . . . . . . . . . . . . . . . a young man

*The play can be performed by a cast of nine men and six women. The roles of MR. GILMER and BOO RADLEY are easily played by one actor, and with a quick change it's possible for the roles of JUDGE TAYLOR and MR. CUNNINGHAM to be played by the same actor.

Extras: TOWNSPEOPLE, FARMERS. If available, extras can also be used as members of Reverend Sykes' CONGREGATION, as the MOB in front of the jailhouse, and as SPECTATORS at the trial.

PLACE: Maycomb, Alabama

TIME: 1935

## Acknowledgments...

This play, of course, begins and ends with Harper Lee's extraordinary Pulitzer Prize book.

Along the way, there has been important help with the play, initially with the editor Maurice Crain and later with two directors.

The first of these is Chris Hayes who produced and directed a production that toured regional theatres in the United Kingdom for nine months and then played seven months at the Mermaid Theatre in London.

Then director Robert Johanson of the Paper Mill Playhouse gave this playwright some creative suggestions that helped shape the final form of the play.

Christopher Sergel

# ACT ONE

SCENE: *The houselights dim and in the darkness there are the soft sounds of birds and in the distance a dog barking.*

*As the stage lights come up it's afternoon and MISS MAUDIE is revealed on her porch, which adjoins the short porch in front of the house of MRS. DUBOSE. MISS MAUDIE has been pruning a plant and she pauses now to listen to the sounds. SCOUT comes in from L, looks back, then crosses to the porch swing where she sits without swinging. She's upset. CAL-PURNIA calls from inside the house.*

CALPURNIA *(off)*. Scout—that you? You out there?

SCOUT *(after a brief pause)*. I'm watching for Atticus. *(SHE starts to swing.)*

CALPURNIA *(off)*. Come in and wash before your father gets home.

SCOUT *(more annoyed)*. In a minute, Calpurnia. *(Muttering.)* Always orders me around.

CALPURNIA *(off)*. You hear me Scout?

SCOUT *(exasperated)*. I have to talk to Atticus. *(Calling.)* Hey, Miss Maudie.

CALPURNIA. Scout!

SCOUT. I'm talking to Miss Maudie.

7

MISS MAUDIE. Do you smell my mimosa? It's like angels' breath.

SCOUT *(uninterested)*. Yessum.

MISS MAUDIE *(trying to encourage her)*. And hear those birds! *(Curiously.)* You do hear the mockingbirds?

SCOUT *(conceding)*. Yessum. *(Maybe SHE's being rude. Feeling SHE must say something.)* When Atticus gave Jem an' me air rifles, he asked us never to shoot mockingbirds.

MISS MAUDIE. And he's right. Mockingbirds just make music. They don't eat up people's gardens; don't nest in corncribs; they don't do one thing but sing their hearts out. That's why it's a sin to kill a mockingbird.

SCOUT. Miss Maudie, this is an old neighborhood, ain't it?

MISS MAUDIE. Been here longer than the town.

SCOUT. No, I mean the folks on our street are all old. Jem an' me's the only children. Mrs. Dubose is close on a hundred and Miss Stephanie's old. So are you, and Atticus—he's ancient!

MISS MAUDIE *(tartly)*. Not being wheeled around yet. Neither is your father.

SCOUT. He's nearly fifty! *(Truly concerned.)* Jem asked him why he was so old an' he said—*(What kind of an answer is this?)*—he got started late.

MISS MAUDIE *(emphatically)*. You're lucky! You and Jem have the benefit of your father's age. If Atticus was thirty, you'd find life quite different.

SCOUT *(equally emphatic)*. I sure would. *(Unhappily.)* Atticus can't *do* anything.

MISS MAUDIE *(exasperated)*. What do you want him to do?

SCOUT *(wouldn't it be wonderful!)*. Drive a dump truck for the county. Run for sheriff. Farm or work in a garage or something else worth mentioning. *(Bitterly.)* Other fathers go hunting, play poker, and they fish.

MISS MAUDIE *(bewildered)*. Seems to me you'd be proud of him.

SCOUT *(a cry)*. Why? He works in a law office and he reads.

BOY'S VOICE *(off.)* Hey, Scout—

SCOUT *(uneasily)*. The way some folks are starting to go on, you'd think he was running a still.

BOY'S VOICE *(off)*. Scout—how come your daddy defends niggers? *(SCOUT has risen and SHE comes to the porch rail, her fists clenched.)*

SCOUT *(shouting back)*. I know it's you, Walter Cunningham. Keep this up 'n' I'll give you another whipping.

BOY'S VOICE *(off, defiant)*. Scout's daddy defends *niggers*!

SCOUT. You gonna take that back, boy?

BOY'S VOICE *(off)*. You gonna make me? My folks say that niggers oughta hang from the water tank.

SCOUT *(starting toward direction of VOICE)*. I'll never speak to you again as long as I live! I hate you an' despise you, an' hope you die tomorrow!

BOY'S VOICE *(off, going)*. Everyone says your daddy's a disgrace!

SCOUT *(close to tears)*. Come back, you coward.

BOY'S VOICE *(off, further away)*. *Everyone*!

SCOUT. *Coward*! *(But HE's gone. SCOUT looks after him, momentarily drained. MISS MAUDIE has the impulse to be helpful, but SHE can't think how.)*

*(CALPURNIA comes out of the house. Probably SHE has heard the shouts.)*

CALPURNIA *(her voice softer than before)*. Scout—I told you to come in and wash up before your father gets home.

SCOUT *(defeated)*. An' I told you—*(Starting.)*—in a minute.

CALPURNIA. Your brother's already washed. *(SCOUT gives her a scowl, then scurries in as CALPURNIA follows her off.)* Why can't you behave as well as Jem?

SCOUT *(off)*. Because he's older'n me and you know it. Ow! The water's too hot.

CALPURNIA *(off)*. Keep scrubbing.

MISS MAUDIE *(conceding)*. Even in 1935, Maycomb, Alabama is already an old town—a tired old town. In rainy weather the streets turn to red slop, grass grows on the sidewalks, the courthouse sags in the square. Old mules hitched to Hoover carts flick flies in the shade. There's no hurry because there's nowhere to go, nothing to buy, and no money to buy it with. Maycomb County had recently been told it had nothing to fear, but fear itself.

*(MISS STEPHANIE has come on during this, pausing to consider the Radley house with disapproval.)*

MISS STEPHANIE. Lack of money is no excuse for the Radleys to let their place go like this. At least they could cut the Johnson grass and rabbit tobacco. *(To MISS MAUDIE.)* But, of course, they're Radleys.

MISS MAUDIE. According to Miss Stephanie, *everybody* in Maycomb has a streak: a drinking streak, a gambling streak, a mean streak, a funny streak.

MISS STEPHANIE. They certainly do. *(Confides. This is delicious.)* No Atkinson minds his own business; every third Merriweather is morbid; the truth is not in the Delafields; all the Bufords walk like that; and if Mrs. Grace sips gin out of Lydia Pinkham bottles, it's nothing unusual—her mother did the same. *(She takes a big breath, ready for the climax.)* As for the *Radleys*—

*(HECK TATE and JUDGE TAYLOR have strolled on during this and the JUDGE unintentionally interrupts.)*

JUDGE TAYLOR. Afternoon, ladies. *(Startled, MISS STEPHANIE freezes.)*

MISS MAUDIE. Judge Taylor...Sheriff.

HECK *(nods to LADIES. Then to business)*. Atticus—you home?

*(CALPURNIA has come out on the porch.)*

CALPURNIA. Not yet, Mr. Tate. Afternoon, Judge Taylor.

HECK. Cal—tell him we were passing by. *(THEY nod and are starting off.)*

CALPURNIA. You want him to call?

JUDGE *(as THEY go. Pleasantly)*. We'll be seeing him anyway.

*(SCOUT is coming back onto the porch drying her hands.)*

CALPURNIA *(passing SCOUT on her way in)*. Change to a clean blouse.

MISS STEPHANIE *(picking up where she left off. In a loud whisper.)* As for the Radleys—

SCOUT *(cutting in)*. Do you think Boo Radley's still alive?

MISS MAUDIE *(calling over)*. His name's Arthur, and he's still alive.

SCOUT. How do you know?

MISS MAUDIE. What a morbid question. I know because I haven't seen him carried out yet.

SCOUT. Jem says maybe he died an' they stuffed him up the chimney.

MISS MAUDIE. He just stays in the house, that's all. Wouldn't you stay in the house if you didn't want to come out?

SCOUT. But I wanta come out.

MISS STEPHANIE *(bursting to get into this. With a relish)*. When that boy was in his teens, he took up with some bad ones from Old Sarum—*(Front.)*—probably drinking stumphole whiskey. They were arrested on charges of disorderly conduct, disturbing the peace, and using abusive and profane language in the presence and hearing of a female. Boo Radley was released to his father, who shut him up in that house and he wasn't seen again for fifteen years.

MISS MAUDIE *(to SCOUT)*. Now she'll tell you what happened fifteen years later.

MISS STEPHANIE *(gives MAUDIE a brief look)*. Boo Radley was sitting in the living room cutting some items from *The Maycomb Tribune* to post in his scrapbook. As his father passed by, Boo drove the scissors into his parent's leg, pulled them out, wiped them on his pants and resumed his activities. Boo was then thirty-three. Mr. Radley said no Radley was going to any insane asylum. So he was kept home where he is till this day. *(Snippily.)* Or Miss Maudie would've seen him carried out.

SCOUT. All my life I've never seen him.

MISS STEPHANIE *(melodramatic).* I saw him. It was stormy, and I woke up in the middle of the night—and there was Boo Radley, his face like a skull—looking in the window, staring at me in my bed!

SCOUT *(fascinated).* What'd you do?

MISS MAUDIE *(helpfully).* She scared him away. *(SCOUT and MISS STEPHANIE look to MISS MAUDIE.)*

SCOUT *(bewildered).* How?

MISS MAUDIE *(with a wicked smile).* She moved over in the bed to make room for him. *(MISS STEPHANIE stares at her for an instant, then gasps.)*

MISS STEPHANIE *(furious).* *You* have a streak, Miss Maudie. *(Starts off, then pauses to fire a parting shot.)* A streak I could not properly describe in front of a young lady.

*(As MISS STEPHANIE exits, MRS. DUBOSE is coming out onto her porch.)*

MISS MAUDIE *(nodding after STEPHANIE, with her smile).* She's right. *(Brightly.)* Afternoon, Mrs. Dubose. *(A grunt in reply does not daunt MISS MAUDIE.)* You must smell my mimosa—*(As SHE goes.)*—angels' breath. *(MRS. DUBOSE is carefully arranging herself in a shawl-draped chair.)*

*(JEM enters L with football.)*

JEM *(calling).* Hey, Scout! *(He tosses the football up, catches it, tucks it under his arm and starts dodging imaginary tacklers.)*

MISS MAUDIE *(front)*. Alabama must be playing in the Rose Bowl with Jem Finch scoring a touchdown. *(She exits.)*

MRS. DUBOSE *(calling to him sharply)*. Where are you going this time of the day, Jeremy Finch? Playing hooky, I suppose. I'll just call up the principal and tell him.

JEM. Aw, it's Saturday, Mrs. Dubose.

MRS. DUBOSE. I wonder if your father knows where you are?

JEM. 'Course he does.

MRS. DUBOSE. Miss Maudie told me you broke down her scuppernong arbour this morning. She's going to tell your father and then you'll wish you'd never seen the light of day!

JEM *(indignant)*. I haven't been near her scuppernong arbour.

MRS. DUBOSE. Don't you contradict me! *(With MRS. DUBOSE calling after him, JEM puts his head down and plunges through the center of the opposing team and bulls his way offstage. MRS. DUBOSE after him.)* If you aren't sent to reform school before next week, my name's not Dubose.

SCOUT *(to herself)*. Why's she so mean?

*(Over the end of the above, the sound of a hymn being sung offstage gradually swells. REVEREND SYKES, a Negro minister, is coming on, possibly followed by a few of the SINGERS, members of his church.)*

MRS. DUBOSE *(sternly)*. Reverend Sykes, please. You must confine your choir to the colored church.

REVEREND SYKES. Excuse us, Mrs. Dubose. We're making a special visit to our parishioners. *(Calling.)* Miss Cal?

*(Annoyed at the singing, MRS. DUBOSE goes inside. CALPURNIA comes out.)*

CALPURNIA. Afternoon, Reverend Sykes.

REVEREND SYKES. It's about Brother Tom Robinson's trouble. We have to do more for his wife and children.

CALPURNIA. Yes, Reverend.

REVEREND SYKES. These are dark days. Days of trials and tribulations. *(The singing begins to swell again. MISS MAUDIE has come out to listen.)*

CALPURNIA. Yes, Reverend.

REVEREND SYKES. The collection for the next three Sundays will go to his wife.

CALPURNIA *(nodding with the music)*. Yes.

REVEREND SYKES. Please encourage *everyone* to bring what they can. Everyone!

SCOUT. Why are you taking up a collection for Tom Robinson's wife?

REVEREND SYKES. To tell the truth, Helen's finding it hard to get work these days.

SCOUT. I know Tom Robinson's done something awful, but why won't folks hire Helen?

REVEREND SYKES. Folks aren't anxious to—*(He hesitates as he sees someone entering. Continuing, dropping his voice.)*—to have anything to do with his family.

*(MAYELLA EWELL has entered, followed by her father, BOB EWELL.)*

MAYELLA *(as they cross the stage)*. Yes, Pa.

BOB EWELL. I told ya—stay outa town right now. Hear?

MAYELLA *(resigned)*. I hear. *(They continue off.)*

MISS MAUDIE *(front)*. Bob Ewell and his daughter, Mayella. Good times or bad they live off the county in a cabin by the garbage dump near a small Negro settlement. *(Smiles wryly.)* All Bob Ewell can hold onto that makes him feel better than his nearest neighbors is that if scrubbed with lye soap in very hot water—his skin is white.

SCOUT *(to REVEREND SYKES, puzzled)*. Why'd you stop talking. Those are just Ewells.

MISS MAUDIE *(as SHE exits. Half to herself)*. I'm not surprised they stopped talking. *(The singing has begun again.)*

REVEREND SYKES. We have a lot of calls to make. Goodbye, Miss Jean Louis.

SCOUT. Call me Scout.

REVEREND SYKES. See you Sunday, Miss Cal.

CALPURNIA. We'll bring all we can.

SCOUT *(after him)*. Bye. *(As they exit, she turns to CALPURNIA. She wants to know.)* What did Tom Robinson do?

CALPURNIA. You mean what do they *say* he did? Old Mr. Bob Ewell accused Tom of raping his girl and had him arrested and put in jail.

SCOUT *(scornfully)*. But everyone in Maycomb knows what kind of folks the Ewells are.

*(JEM has come back on, hearing the last of this.)*

JEM. What's the singing?

SCOUT. Jem—what's rape?

JEM *(after short consideration)*. Ask Cal.

CALPURNIA *(even shorter consideration)*. I think you better ask your father. *(Going.)* We'll be eating soon.

SCOUT. I'd just like to know—

*(SCOUT stops as DILL is entering.)*

SCOUT. Hey—

DILL. Hey, yourself. I'm Charles Baker Harris. I can read.

JEM. So what?

DILL. I just thought you'd like to know. Folks call me Dill. I'm staying with my Aunt Rachel.

SCOUT *(critically)*. You're sort of puny.

DILL *(defensively)*. I'm little, but I'm old.

SCOUT *(curious)*. How old's your father?

DILL. I haven't got one.

SCOUT. Is he dead?

DILL. No.

SCOUT. Then if he's not dead, you've got one, haven't you? *(DILL is embarrassed.)*

JEM. Never mind her, Dill.

SCOUT *(persisting)*. If his father isn't dead, how can he say he hasn't got one? How...*(SHE is interrupted by JEM who grabs her arm.)*

JEM. Scout! The Radley Place!

*(SCOUT stops at his tone, and turns to look with him at the Radley door, which is opening. NATHAN RADLEY, a pale, thin, leathery man is coming out.)*

SCOUT *(with relief)*. Nathan Radley.

JEM *(clearing throat nervously)*. Hidy-do, Mr. Nathan.

NATHAN *(preoccupied)*. Afternoon. *(Exits.)*

SCOUT *(explaining to DILL. Hushed)*. Boo Radley's older brother. *(Ominously.)* Boo Radley's in there—all by himself—an' he hasn't come out in twenty, thirty years.

DILL. Thirty years!

JEM. When old Mr. Radley died, some folks thought Boo'd have to come out, but Nathan moved in and took his father's place.

DILL. Wonder what he does. Looks like he'd stick his head out the door sometime.

JEM. I think he comes out when it's pitch dark. Azaleas wilt 'cause he breathes on them. Nobody touches a pecan that falls off the Radley pecan tree...it'll *kill* you. I've seen his tracks in our backyard many a morning, and one night I heard him scratching on the back screen.

DILL. Wonder what he looks like?

JEM. *(professionally)*. Judging from his tracks, he's about six-and-a-half feet tall, he eats raw squirrels and any cats he can catch. What teeth he has are yellow and rotten. His eyes pop and most of the time he drools.

DILL *(with decision)*. Let's make him come out.

SCOUT *(shocked)*. Make Boo Radley come out?

JEM. If you want to get yourself killed, all you have to do is go up and knock on that door.

DILL *(challenging)*. You're scared—too scared to put your big toe in the front yard.

JEM. Ain't scared, just respectful.

DILL. I dare you.

JEM. *(trapped)*. You dare me? *(JEM turns to look at the house apprehensively.)*

SCOUT. Don't go near it, Jem. If you get killed—what with Atticus so old—what would become of me? *(JEM does not respond.)*

DILL *(impatiently)*. Well?

JEM. Don't hurry me. *(JEM starts slowly toward the house.)*

DILL. Scout and me's right behind you. *(As JEM continues toward the Radley house, SCOUT and DILL follow, SCOUT pausing beside the tree. JEM hesitates. SCOUT notices something in a knothole in the tree and takes it. In a hushed voice.)* Someone's at the window! Look at the curtains! *(The curtains have been pulled slightly to the side, and now they fall back into place.)*

JEM *(horrified)*. He was watching! He saw me!

SCOUT *(absently putting a piece of chewing gum in her mouth.)* Don't *ever* do that.

JEM (considering her). Where'd you get the chewing gum?

SCOUT *(as SHE chews, SHE nods toward the tree)*. It was sticking in the knothole.

JEM *(shocked)*. That tree? Spit it out! Right now!

SCOUT *(obeying, but indignant)*. I was just getting the flavour.

JEM *(grimly)*. Suppose Boo Radley put it there? Suppose it's poison? You go gargle!

SCOUT *(shaking her head)*. It'd take the taste outa my mouth.

DILL *(still concentrating on the Radley house)*. Let's throw a pebble against the door—and as soon as he sticks his head out, say we want to buy him an ice cream. *(Logically.)* That'll seem friendly. Maybe he'd feel better.

SCOUT. How do you know he don't feel good now?

DILL *(concerned)*. How'd you feel if you'd been shut up for a hundred years with nothing but cats to eat? *(Searching about.)* 'Course if you'd rather *I* throw the pebble—

JEM (*disgusted*). Better leave it to me. (*JEM apparently picks up a pebble.*)

SCOUT (*worried*). You're not going to throw a stone at the Radley house!

JEM (*to DILL, as HE winds up to throw*). I guess I just have to show you—(*HE is stopped by an authoritative voice from off.*)

ATTICUS (*off*). Jem! (*JEM stops and they ALL look toward the direction of the VOICE off.*)

SCOUT. Atticus!

(*ATTICUS, carrying an old briefcase and wearing his "office" clothes, comes on. He's tall, quietly impressive, reserved, civilized and nearly fifty. He wears glasses and because of the poor sight in his left eye, looks with his right eye when he wants to see something well.*)

ATTICUS (*trying to take in the situation, curiously*). Just what were you about to do, Jem?

JEM. Nothin', sir.

ATTICUS (*unwilling to be put off*). I don't want any of that. Tell me.

JEM. We were—(*Assuming responsibility.*)—I was going to throw a pebble—to get Boo Radley to come out.

ATTICUS. *Why?*

DILL. Because—sir. (*As ATTICUS turns to him, DILL clears his throat. Explaining quickly.*) My name's Charles Baker Harris—people call me Dill. I'm here visiting my Aunt Rachel. (*Lamely.*) We thought Mr. Radley might enjoy us...

ATTICUS *(gravely)*. I see. *(Turning back to JEM with decision.)* Son, I'm going to tell you something and tell you one time. Don't bother that man.

SCOUT. But why doesn't he ever—

ATTICUS *(cutting in)*. What Mr. Radley does is his own business. If he wants to stay inside his own house, he has the right to stay inside—free from the attention of inquisitive children. How would you like it if I barged into your rooms at night without knocking?

JEM. That's different.

ATTICUS. Is it?

JEM. Because we're not crazy.

ATTICUS. What Mr. Radley does might seem peculiar to us, but it does *not* seem peculiar to him.

JEM *(protesting)*. Anyone who stays inside all the time and never—

ATTICUS *(cutting in)*. But that's *his* decision. *(Considering them.)* There's something I'd like to ask. If you'll do it, you'll get along a lot better with *all* kinds. You see, you never really understand a person until you consider things from his point of view.

JEM. Sir?

ATTICUS. Until you climb into his skin and walk around in it.

JEM *(incredulous)*. You want us to consider things from Boo Radley's point of view?

DILL *(impatiently)*. He means—everyone.

SCOUT. You stay outa this.

ATTICUS *(smiling)*. Mr. Harris is right. But I expect I'm asking too much. There's Cunningham.

*(With ATTICUS diverted, DILL speaks confidentially to JEM and SCOUT, with a nod toward the Radley house.)*

DILL. I've got a much better plan. *(Starting to go.)* See you.

*(MR. CUNNINGHAM, a farmer, carrying a sack, is coming on as DILL runs past him.)*

ATTICUS *(calling)*. Afternoon. *(Aside to JEM and SCOUT, using DILL's confidential tone and nod.)* Regardless of any plans, you're to stay away from that house unless invited.

MR. CUNNINGHAM *(holding out the sack)*. This is for you, Mr. Finch. Turnip Greens.

ATTICUS *(accepting the sack gravely)*. Thank you very much.

MR. CUNNINGHAM. I'd like to pay cash for your services, but between the mortgage and the entailment—

ATTICUS. This is just fine. Jem, please take this sack to Cal. *(JEM takes sack and goes inside.)* I'd say your bill is settled.

MR. CUNNINGHAM *(doubtfully)*. You put in a lot of time.

ATTICUS. Let's see now. You left a load of stove wood in the backyard, then a sack of hickory nuts. At Christmas there was a crate of smilax and holly. Now a bag of turnip greens. I'm more than paid.

MR. CUNNINGHAM. If you say so.

SCOUT. Your boy's in my class at school, Mr. Cunningham. *(Uneasily, as SHE recalls.)* We had a disagreement the other day.

MR. CUNNINGHAM *(smiling)*. I have a few with that boy myself, little lady.

SCOUT *(concerned)*. I didn't actually beat him up bad.

MR. CUNNINGHAM *(amused)*. If he can't defend himself against a girl, he'll just have to take it. *(To ATTICUS as HE goes.)* Much obliged, Mr. Finch.

ATTICUS *(after him)*. Any time I can be of help.

SCOUT *(curious)*. Why does he pay with stove wood and turnip greens?

ATTICUS. Because that's the only way he can.

SCOUT. Are *we* poor, Atticus?

ATTICUS. We are indeed.

SCOUT. As poor as the Cunninghams?

ATTICUS. Not exactly. The Cunninghams are country folks and the depression hits them hardest. *(Curious.)* What was your trouble with my client's boy?

SCOUT. He said some things I didn't like. *(Shrugs.)* I rubbed his nose in the dirt.

ATTICUS. That's not very ladylike. What'd he say?

*(JEM is coming back onto the porch with his football.)*

SCOUT. Things. And I think we should have a talk. I've been watching for you to get home because—*(SHE is interrupted by JEM, who is cocking his arm to pass the football.)*

JEM. Atticus! Catch!

ATTICUS *(making no move)*. Hang onto it, Son. Not today.

JEM *(coming down off the porch)*. Atticus, will you be going out for the Methodists? For the football game?

ATTICUS. What game?

JEM *(eagerly)*. It won't be till fall, but everyone's talking about it already. It's for fund-raising. The Methodists challenged the Baptists to a game of touch football.

ATTICUS *(smiling)*. 'Afraid I wouldn't be of much help, Jem.

JEM. Everybody's father is playing.

ATTICUS *(going up onto the porch)*. Except yours.

JEM *(insisting)*. Every other father—

ATTICUS *(cheerfully)*. I'd break my neck.

JEM. It's *touch*.

ATTICUS. I'm too old for that sort of thing.

JEM *(unhappily, taking a breath)*. Sir—would you have time to show Scout 'n me how to shoot our air rifles? Later, I mean?

ATTICUS*(sorry to be a disappointment)*. I've told you— you'll have to wait for your Uncle Jack. *(Encouragingly.)* He'll *really* show you. *(ATTICUS seems to be missing the point.)*

JEM. Couldn't *you* show us?

ATTICUS *(as a simple statement of fact)*. I'm not interested in guns.

JEM. You're not interested in *anything*! *(With all his strength, JEM throws the football offstage. ATTICUS and JEM face each other for a moment.)*

ATTICUS *(quietly)*. I think you better go get your football. *(JEM, frustrated, turns and rushes off.)*

SCOUT. Atticus—*(ATTICUS turns to focus on SCOUT.)* Tell me—what's rape? *(ATTICUS considers SCOUT for a moment. Then he sits on the swing. Takes a breath.)*

ATTICUS. Rape is carnal knowledge of a female by force.

SCOUT. If that's all it is, why did Calpurnia dry up when I asked her? *(Takes a breath.)* Atticus, do you defend niggers?

ATTICUS *(startled)*. Of course I do. Don't say 'nigger,' Scout. That's common.

SCOUT. 'S what everybody at school says.

ATTICUS. From now on it'll be everybody less one.

SCOUT. Do all lawyers defend n—Negroes?

ATTICUS. They do.

SCOUT *(exasperated)*. Then why do the kids at school make it sound like you're doin' somethin' awful?

ATTICUS. You aren't old enough to understand some things yet, Scout, but there's been a lot of high talk around town that I shouldn't do much about defending Tom Robinson. *(Firmly.)* But I'm going to defend that man.

SCOUT. If they say you shouldn't, why are you doing it?

ATTICUS *(considering this)*. The main reason: If I didn't defend him, I couldn't really have much respect for myself, could I? *(ATTICUS looks at SCOUT and smiles.)* I couldn't even tell you or Jem not to do something again.

SCOUT. You mean Jem and me wouldn't have to mind you any more?

ATTICUS. That's about right.

SCOUT. Why?

ATTICUS. Because I could never *ask* you to mind me again. *(Frankly.)* To tell the truth, I'd hoped to get through life without a case of this kind, but Judge Taylor pointed at me and said, 'You're it.'

SCOUT. Are we going to win it?

ATTICUS. No, honey. Come here, Scout.

SCOUT. Then, why—*(She gets into his lap.)*

ATTICUS. Simply because we were licked a hundred years before we started is no reason for us not to *try* to win.

SCOUT. You sound like some old Confederate veteran.

ATTICUS. Only we aren't fighting Yankees. We'll be fighting our friends. But remember this, no matter how bitter things get, they're still our friends and this is still our home.

*(MISS MAUDIE comes on her porch with a watering can.)*

SCOUT *(confused).* Is there something you want me to do, Atticus?

ATTICUS *(nodding).* Just hold your head high, and keep those fists down. And I hope you can get through what's coming without catching Maycomb's usual disease. Why reasonable people go stark raving mad when anything involving a Negro comes up is something I can't pretend to understand.

SCOUT. The Tom Robinson case must be pretty important.

ATTICUS *(speaking quietly).* It's about right and wrong.

SCOUT *(concerned for him).* Suppose you're wrong about it?

ATTICUS. How's that?

SCOUT. Most people think that they're right and you're wrong.

ATTICUS. They're entitled to think that, and they're entitled to full respect for their opinions.

CALPURNIA *(off).* Dinner's ready.

ATTICUS *(getting up from swing).* But one thing does *not* abide by majority rule, honey—*(As he goes in.)*—it's your conscience.

*(SCOUT, perplexed, looks after him. Then turns as a chastened JEM comes on holding his football. He pauses to look back casually.)*

SCOUT. Jem, I was talking with Atticus about the Tom Robinson case.

JEM. Dinner ready yet?

SCOUT *(annoyed)*. Yes. What Atticus said—*(Noticing JEM looking off. She looks, too.)* Why do folks slow down as they go past?

VOICE *(off)*. Yonder's some Finches.

ANOTHER VOICE *(off)*. Them's his chill'un.

ANOTHER VOICE *(off)*. For all *he* cares, niggers c'n run wild'n rape white women! *(SCOUT, ready to explode, has clenched her fists.)*

MISS MAUDIE *(calls)*. Miss Jean Louise—

SCOUT *(tight)*. Yes, Miss Maudie?

MISS MAUDIE *(gently)*. Thought I heard Calpurnia call you for dinner.

SCOUT. But—*(She gestures in the direction of the VOICES.)* That's—ugly!

JEM. C'mon, Scout.

SCOUT *(as she goes. An accusation)*. I guess the Tom Robinson case isn't as new to you as it is to me.

MISS MAUDIE *(looking after them. Agreeing with SCOUT)*. I guess not. Tension in the town about the approaching trial beginning to get drum tight. And the talk beginning to get ugly. A few weeks later, something happened that made Atticus even more of a puzzle—but it had nothing to do with the trial—it had to do with a liver-colored birddog named Tim.

*(Lights are up, and JEM and SCOUT are coming back on with JEM pulling SCOUT.)*

SCOUT *(protesting)*. *Why* do I have to come home?

JEM. Because I tell you. That old dog from down yonder is sick. *(Calling.)* Cal, can you come out a minute?

SCOUT. It's only Tim, and he's gone lopsided, that's all.

*(CALPURNIA comes out onto the porch, wiping her hands on a tea towel.)*

CALPURNIA. What is it, Jem? I can't come out every time you want me.

JEM. Somethin' wrong with that old dog down yonder.

CALPURNIA *(sighing)*. I can't wrap up any dog's foot right now.

JEM. He's sick, Cal. Somethin' wrong with him.

CALPURNIA *(finally interested)*. Tryin' to catch his tail?

JEM. No, he's doin' like this. *(JEM gulps, like a goldfish, hunching his shoulders and twisting his torso, while CALPURNIA watches narrowly.)*

CALPURNIA *(her voice hardening)*. You tellin' me a story, Jem Finch?

JEM. No, Cal. And he's coming this way.

CALPURNIA. You two get in off the street. *(CALPURNIA hurries inside.)*

JEM *(to SCOUT)*. Come on.

SCOUT *(reluctantly coming up onto the porch with JEM)*. He's not even in sight.

CALPURNIA *(off. Loud and anxious; on a telephone just inside the porch door)*. Operator, hello—Miss Eula May, ma'am? Please gimme Mr. Finch's office—right away!

SCOUT *(to JEM)*. You started something.

CALPURNIA *(off. On the telephone, half-shouting)*. Mr. Finch, this is Cal. There's a mad dog down the street a piece. Jem says he's comin' this way! Yes—yessir— yes! *(SHE hangs up.)*

JEM *(calling in)*. What's Atticus say?

CALPURNIA *(off, calling back)*. In a minute. *(SHE rattles the telephone hook and then speaks loudly again.)* Miss Eula May. I'm through talking to Mr. Finch. Listen, can you call Miss Crawford and whoever's got a phone on this street and tell 'em a mad dog's comin'? Please ma'am...hurry! *(CALPURNIA comes back on porch.)*

SCOUT. What about the Radleys? They got a phone? *(SHE starts toward the Radley house.)*

CALPURNIA. Both of you—inside the house and stay inside! *(SHE pauses to look off.)* That's Tim gone mad all right! *(SHE comes after SCOUT who has stopped to shout at the silent Radley house.)*

SCOUT. He's comin' now, Mr. Radley!

CALPURNIA *(giving SCOUT a fierce swat on the seat).* Get inside! *(SCOUT is muttering bitterly as she goes up onto the porch.)*

SCOUT. You always pick on me.

CALPURNIA. You stay back! *(CALPURNIA races up on the Radley porch where SHE starts banging on the door, at the same time casting about nervous glances.)* Mr. Nathan—Mr. Boo! Mad dog's comin'! Mad dog's comin'! Hear me? Don't come outside. Mad dog!

SCOUT. She's supposed to go around in back.

JEM. Don't matter this time. *(Suddenly tense as HE watches.)* I see him! There he is! Cal! *(CALPURNIA herds them ahead of her onto the porch, anxiously looking back. JEM is considering the situation offstage again.)* Old Tim's walkin' like his right legs are shorter than his left legs. *(They ALL lean forward to watch. From off there is the sound of an automobile approaching and coming to a stop.)*

SCOUT *(noticing offstage).* He brought the sheriff—

JEM. *Someone* has to stop Old Tim.

*(ATTICUS comes on with HECK TATE, who carries a heavy rifle.)*

JEM (*going down to join them*). Atticus—he's over there behind...

ATTICUS. Stay on the porch, Son.

CALPURNIA. Back behind the Radley pecan trees.

HECK. Not runnin', is he, Cal?

CALPURNIA. He's in the twitchin' stage, Mr. Heck. (*HECK watches carefully as HE advances a few steps.*)

HECK. Usually they go in a straight line, but you never can tell.

ATTICUS (*following behind HECK*). The slope will probably bring him back onto the road.

SCOUT (*to CALPURNIA*). I thought mad dogs foamed at the mouth and jumped at your throat.

CALPURNIA. Hush.

ATTICUS (*softly*). There he is.

SCOUT. He just looks sick.

HECK (*aside to ATTICUS*). He's got it all right, Mr. Finch.

JEM (*calling*). Is he looking for a place to die, Mr. Heck?

HECK (*over his shoulder*). Far from dead, Jem. He hasn't got started yet.

ATTICUS. He's within range, Heck. You better get him before he goes down a side street. Lord knows who's around the corner. (*Calling back.*) Cal—

CALPURNIA (*understanding; to JEM and SCOUT*). Inside the house—both of you.

JEM (*temporizing*). If he gets closer...

SCOUT (*clutching the porch rail tightly with both hands*). I don't go in till he goes in.

JEM. I wanta watch the sheriff!

HECK (*turns and offers the rifle to ATTICUS*). You take him, Mr. Finch. You do it.

ATTICUS (*urgently*). Don't waste time, Heck! Go on!

HECK. Mr. Finch—this is a one-shot job.

ATTICUS *(vehemently)*. Don't just stand there, Heck!

HECK *(frantic)*. Look where he is! For God's sake, Mr. Finch! I can't shoot that well and you know it.

ATTICUS. I haven't shot a gun in thirty years.

HECK *(shoves the rifle to ATTICUS' hands)*. I'd feel mighty comfortable if you did now. *(Holding the rifle, ATTICUS decides to accept the responsibility and, watching carefully, HE moves forward several steps.)*

SCOUT *(bewildered)*. What's he gonna do with the rifle?

JEM *(concerned, calling)*. Mr. Heck—*(HECK gestures JEM away.)*

*(ATTICUS has taken off his glasses, and still keeping watch, HE drops them on the street. HE rubs one eye and blinks. Then his body goes tense as HE focuses totally on the mad dog offstage.)*

CALPURNIA *(her hands to her cheeks)*. Sweet Jesus, help us.

*(ATTICUS works the bolt action, apparently slamming a cartridge into the chamber, raises the rifle quickly, and fires.)*

HECK *(a shout)*. Got him! *(Happy and relieved, as HE hurries off.)* You got him!

ATTICUS *(after him)*. Yes, but I think I was a little to the right. *(Muttering as HE picks up his glasses.)* If I had my drothers, I'd take a shotgun!

*(HECK is re-entering.)*

HECK. Dead as a doornail. *(As though it's news.)* Just a *little* to the right.

ATTICUS *(handing the rifle back to HECK.)* Always was.

*(Porch doors are opening. MISS MAUDIE is cautiously coming out, as MISS STEPHANIE is also coming on.)*

HECK. I'll have someone come down with a pickup and take him away.

ATTICUS *(stops JEM and SCOUT, who are coming down off the porch).* You stay where you are.

HECK. You haven't forgot, Mr. Finch. They say it never leaves you.

JEM *(calling).* Atticus—

ATTICUS. Yes, Jem?

JEM. I didn't know.

MISS MAUDIE *(from her porch).* I saw that, One-Shot-Finch. *(ATTICUS shakes his head at her and turns back to JEM.)*

ATTICUS. Jem—you and your sister stay away from that dog. He's just as dangerous dead as alive.

JEM. Yes, sir. Atticus?

ATTICUS. What, Son?

HECK *(amused at JEM's hesitation).* What's the matter, boy, can't you talk? Didn't you know your daddy's—

ATTICUS. Hush, Heck. Let's get back to town.

HECK. What's your hurry now? *(Good-humored teasing.)* Have to get back to workin' your speeches for the trial?

ATTICUS *(as THEY go, wryly).* Don't remind me. *(THEY go off. CALPURNIA goes inside the house.)*

MISS STEPHANIE. Maybe Tim wasn't really mad. Maybe he was just full of fleas—and Atticus Finch shot him dead.

MISS MAUDIE. If that Tim was still comin' up the street, maybe you'd be singing a different tune.

MISS STEPHANIE *(agreeing, reluctantly)*. Maybe I would. *(As SHE is going back off.)* I'll admit I felt safer when I saw Atticus take the rifle.

JEM *(still in shock)*. Did you see him, Scout? He did it so quick.

MISS MAUDIE *(with a wicked smile)*. Well, now, Miss Scout. Still think your father can't do anything? Still ashamed of him?

SCOUT *(meekly)*. No, ma'am.

MISS MAUDIE. Forgot to mention the other day that he was the deadest shot in Maycomb County.

JEM. Dead shot—

MISS MAUDIE. When he was a boy his nickname was Ol' One-Shot. Something for you to think about, Jem Finch.

JEM. But he never said anything about it.

SCOUT. Wonder why he never goes huntin' now.

MISS MAUDIE. If your father's anything, he's civilized. Marksmanship like that's a gift from God. I think maybe he put his gun down when he realized God had given him an unfair advantage.

SCOUT. Looks like he'd be proud of it.

MISS MAUDIE *(going)*. People like your father never bother about pride in their gifts.

*(MISS MAUDIE re-enters her house. MRS. DUBOSE is coming out onto her porch.)*

SCOUT *(filled with anticipation)*. Will I have something to tell 'em at school on Monday!

JEM. Don't know if we should say anything about it.

SCOUT *(coming down off the porch)*. I'd like to find the Cunningham boy right now! Ain't everybody's daddy the deadest shot in Maycomb County.

JEM *(following her)*. I reckon if he'd wanted us to know, he'da told us.

SCOUT. Maybe it just slipped his mind.

JEM. Naw, it's something you wouldn't understand. *(Blazing with this new pride.)* We don't have to talk about it any mor'n he does—but we know! *(To the sky.)* An' I don't care if he's a hundred years old!

SCOUT *(calling out)*. Hey, Mrs. Dubose! Did you see my father—

MRS. DUBOSE. Don't say 'hey' to me, you ugly girl! You say 'Good afternoon, Mrs. Dubose.' You should be in a dress and camisole, young lady. If somebody doesn't change your ways, you'll grow up waiting on tables. A Finch waiting on tables at the O.K. Cafe—hah! *(SCOUT, upset, reaches out and takes JEM's hand.)*

SCOUT *(frightened and hurt, hushed aside)*. What's the matter with her? Why's she so hateful?

JEM *(aside to her, whispering)*. Come on, Scout. Don't pay any attention. Just hold your head high—be a gentleman. *(SCOUT decides to make the effort, and THEY start walking again. However MRS. DUBOSE will not let them alone.)*

MRS. DUBOSE. A lovelier lady than your mother never lived. It's shocking the way Atticus Finch lets her children run wild. *(JEM hesitates.)*

SCOUT *(whispering)*. I'm with you.

JEM *(whispering back)*. We'll keep walking.

MRS. DUBOSE. Not only a Finch waiting on tables, but one in the courthouse, lawing for niggers! *(JEM, stung hard, stops short.)*

SCOUT *(whispering anxiously)*. Let's keep goin', Jem.

MRS. DUBOSE *(as SHE's going back inside)*. What's the world come to with the Finches going against their raising? *(Her parting shot.)* Your father's no better than the trash he works for! He's a nigger lover! *(With this SHE completes her exit, leaving SCOUT hurt and JEM stunned.)*

JEM *(gasping)*. I'll—I'll fix her!

SCOUT. Hold your head high, Jem, an'—

JEM. She has no right—

SCOUT *(trying to hold him)*. Jem—

JEM *(shoving her hands away)*. Just because Atticus—I'm sick and tired—everybody—*everybody*! *(JEM races up onto MRS. DUBOSE's porch, where HE starts tearing up the potted flowers there.)*

SCOUT *(frantic)*. Jem! Come back!

JEM *(shouting back)*. Go home! Stay outa this! *(As the shocked SCOUT feels her way back toward her porch, JEM turns, having completed the destruction of MRS. DUBOSE's porch flowers, and rushes off, apparently intent on further objects for his fury.)*

SCOUT *(after him; a cry)*. Jem!

*(But JEM, past hearing, has gone. Frightened, SCOUT goes back onto her porch, from where SHE watches anxiously. DILL, dressed in different clothes—dusty and untidy—comes on.)*

DILL *(subdued)*. Hey, Scout.

SCOUT *(DILL's presence only half-registering)*. Jem's outa control! He's gone mad! *(Looking back.)* He's knocking the tops off every camellia bush Mrs. Dubose owns!

DILL *(impressed)*. Thought Jem had a slow fuse.

SCOUT. Not anymore. He's gone crazy.

DILL. From people sayin' things about your father?

SCOUT. Yes—Mrs. Dubose—*(Stops herself, curiously.)* How'd you know? *(DILL shrugs. Eager for DILL to know.)* We found out somethin' about Atticus today—somethin' special.

DILL *(not surprised)*. About time.

SCOUT *(bursting with it)*. He's the deadest shot in May-comb!

DILL *(this is not what DILL expects. Disappointed)*. That's what you found out?

SCOUT *(nodding)*. It's the truth. So it doesn't matter *what* folks say.

DILL. Wouldn't matter anyway. *(SCOUT becomes aware that THEY are not quite talking about the same thing. SHE considers him.)*

SCOUT. What are you doing here? I thought you'd been taken back to stay with your folks in Meridian?

DILL *(uneasily)*. I—I was.

SCOUT. Then how in the Sam Hill—

DILL. It's—you see—

SCOUT *(as his appearance finally registers)*. You're all mussed 'n' dusty.

DILL. 'Course I am. *(HE takes a quick breath.)* I have a new father, and he doesn't like me—so he had me bound in chains and left to die in the basement. But I was secretly kept alive on raw field beans by a passing farmer who heard my cries for help.

SCOUT. If you were chained up in the basement—

DILL. The good man poked a bushel of beans to me—pod by pod—through the ventilator!

*(During this, JEM is coming back on at the point where HE went off. Aghast at himself, HE is moving slowly toward the porch, not yet noticed by the OTHERS.)*

SCOUT *(hooked)*. Lucky for you that good man was passing.

DILL *(sure of himself now)*. I worked myself free—pulling the chains from the wall. Then I wandered out of Meridian where I discovered a small animal show—and they hired me to wash the camel.

SCOUT. How do you go about washing a—

DILL *(pressing on)*. Suddenly my sense of direction told me I was just across the river from Maycomb. *(HE gulps a quick breath.)* What I did then—*(JEM has come up on the last of this, still unnoticed.)*

JEM *(cutting in)*. How *did* you get here, Dill?

DILL *(sighing; undramatic)*. I took thirteen dollars from my mother's purse and caught the nine o'clock train from Meridian.

JEM. Why'd you run off?

DILL. Didn't run off. Decided I'd come back here, that's all.

SCOUT. You want to stay with your Aunt Rachel?

DILL. I want to stay here.

SCOUT. With us?

JEM *(grim)*. We're gonna have a hot summer.

DILL. I don't care.

*(ATTICUS is hurrying on.)*

SCOUT *(warningly)*. Jem—*(ATTICUS walks past them over to the front of the DUBOSE house, and for a moment HE considers it.)*

JEM *(aside to DILL, nervously)*. Maybe you better come back later.

DILL *(hushed)*. I'm not going. *(ATTICUS turns and walks back toward the GROUP.)*

SCOUT *(bravely)*. Look at this, Atticus—we've got a visitor. Here's Dill—come back from Meridian. *(Trying to fill the awkward silence.)* He knows how to wash a camel.

ATTICUS *(gravely acknowledging him)*. Dill.

DILL *(swallowing)*. Sir.

ATTICUS *(a suggestion of winter in his voice)*. Jem—I had a phone call a few minutes ago. Are you responsible for the damage to those flowers?

JEM. Yes, sir.

ATTICUS. Why'd you do it?

JEM *(softly)*. Mrs. Dubose said you lawed for niggers.

ATTICUS *(getting it straight)*. And that's why you destroyed her garden?

JEM *(swallowing)*. Yes, sir.

ATTICUS. Son, I have no doubt you've been annoyed by your contemporaries about me lawing for niggers, as you say, but to do something like this to a sick old lady is inexcusable. I strongly advise you to go over and have a talk with Mrs. Dubose.

JEM *(startled)*. Talk to her!

ATTICUS. Right now.

JEM. But—

ATTICUS. Go on, Jem.

SCOUT. But—sir—

ATTICUS *(stopping her)*. Scout.

JEM *(getting himself together)*. All right. I'll go talk to her.

ATTICUS *(unmoved)*. Come straight home afterwards.

*(JEM goes toward the Dubose house like a man walking bravely to his execution. During the following speeches, he goes up to her door, knocks, and is let in.)*

SCOUT *(to ATTICUS)*. All he was doin' was standin' up for you!

ATTICUS *(as HE looks after JEM)*. Never thought Jem'd be the one to lose his head. *(Turning toward SCOUT.)* Thought I'd have more trouble with you.

SCOUT. Why do we have to keep our heads anyway? Nobody at school has to keep his head about anything.

ATTICUS *(not happy about it)*. You'll soon have to be keeping your head about far worse things. *(Turning to DILL.)* Your Aunt Rachel didn't mention you were coming back.

SCOUT. She doesn't know.

DILL. Please, Mr. Finch—don't tell her I'm here.

ATTICUS. Don't tell her—

SCOUT. He's run away.

DILL. *Don't* make me go back, sir.

ATTICUS. Just let me get this straight—

DILL. If you make me go back, I'll run away again.

ATTICUS. Whoa, Son.

SCOUT. He's been living on raw beans.

DILL *(nervously)*. Scout—

ATTICUS. Let me do a little telephoning. *(Not letting DILL interrupt.)* I'll ask if you could spend the night— perhaps stay a few days.

DILL *(hopefully)*. Would you, sir?

ATTICUS *(as HE goes inside)*. Maybe Scout can get you something to go with the raw beans.

DILL *(after him)*. Oh, I'm fine. Not hungry at all. *(ATTICUS smiles as HE enters the house.)*

SCOUT *(regarding DILL critically).* I'd think you'd be starving. *(DILL shrugs. Her suspicions grow.)* Was your father really hateful like you said?

DILL *(unhappily).* That wasn't it, he—they just wasn't interested in me.

SCOUT. You're not telling me right. Your folks couldn't do without you.

DILL. Yes, they can, They get on a lot better without me. They stay gone most of the time, and when they're home, they're always off by themselves. And—I can't help them any. *(Being fair.)* They're not mean. They buy me everything I want, but then it's—*(Imitating a man's voice.)*—now-you've-got-it-go-play-with-it.

SCOUT. They must need you. Why, Atticus couldn't get along a day without my help and advice.

DILL *(struggling with an idea).* The special thing about your father—it isn't that he's a dead shot, it's—

SCOUT *(highly critical).* He made Jem go over to Mrs. Dubose.

DILL. Don't you see why he did that?

SCOUT *(unimpressed).* Because it's his way.

DILL *(agreeing).* And Jem'll be all right. *(Trying to catch her interest.)* If I get to stay a few days, I have a new plan for bringing out Boo Radley.

SCOUT. Wanta see what else I found in the knothole of that tree? *(Taking them out.)* Two Indian head pennies —all slicked up.

DILL. Who would leave valuable Indian head pennies?

SCOUT *(turning to look at the Radley house).* Why do you reckon Boo Radley's never run off?

DILL. Maybe he doesn't have anywhere to run off to. *(Back to business.)* For my plan to get him out we'll need a box of lemon drops. I'll put one just outside his door—and then a row of them down the street.

*(ATTICUS is coming back onto the porch, but DILL is too wrapped up in his scheme to see him.)*

DILL. When he thinks he's safe, he'll come out to pick up the lemon drops. *(DILL's pantomiming is leading him toward the still unseen ATTICUS.)* Then he'll notice the next one—then on to the next—he'll follow like an ant —then another—then—*(The place for the next imaginary sweet is occupied by ATTICUS' shoes. DILL stops and looks up.)*

ATTICUS *(smiling)*. That's a lot of lemon drops.

DILL *(uneasily)*. We were foolin', sir.

ATTICUS. You've been the subject of considerable conversation.

DILL. What'd Aunt Rachel say?

ATTICUS. At first it came under the heading of: 'His folks must be out of their minds worrying,' and she ended with 'Reckon he can stay on for tonight anyway.'

DILL *(delighted)*. Hey! *(To SCOUT.)* Hear that!

ATTICUS. But I thought I'd better speak to your parents, so I called them, too.

DILL *(suddenly serious)*. What'd they say?

ATTICUS. Couldn't 've been more agreeable. *(Smiling.)* They said you could stay on for as long as you're not in the way. *(SCOUT gives a gasp of pleasure.)*

DILL *(subdued)*. I see.

SCOUT. Great! Isn't that great?

DILL *(with an effort)*. Sure it is. *(To ATTICUS, trying to draw him out.)* Guess they were looking all over Meridian for me.

ATTICUS (*shaking his head and smiling*). No, they thought you were probably stuck at some picture show.

DILL (*disappointed, but smiling back*). Generally, they'd be right, too.

ATTICUS (*becoming aware of DILL's problem*). We'll be going through quite a difficult time, Dill. It'll be good having you with us.

DILL. Do you mean—

ATTICUS. It'll be a help having you here. There's a cot in Jem's room.

(*HECK TATE is coming on.*)

DILL. *Thank* you, sir. Thank you *very* much.

HECK (*calling*). Mr. Finch.

ATTICUS. More company. Come on up, Heck.

HECK (*reserved*). Rather speak with you down here.

ATTICUS (*thoughtfully*). Oh?

SCOUT (*aside to ATTICUS*). What is it?

ATTICUS. Only two reasons why grown men talk in the front yard—death or politics. (*Calling.*) Which is it, Heck?

HECK (*wryly*). Could be a little of both, Mr. Finch.

ATTICUS (*considering this*). Then we'd better talk. (*HE pauses. To SCOUT.*) Maybe you and Dill can give Calpurnia a hand.

SCOUT. I want to know what's happening.

ATTICUS (*firmly*). You'll give Calpurnia a hand. (*Glancing toward him.*) Dill? (*DILL takes hold of SCOUT's arm, as ATTICUS crosses over to HECK.*)

SCOUT (*jerking her arm free*). Don't get any ideas you can boss me, too! (*SCOUT crosses over to the porch swing.*)

DILL *(following, apologetically).* They have business. *(HECK has turned aside and speaks confidentially to ATTICUS.)*

HECK. They moved Tom Robinson to the county jail this afternoon. I don't look for trouble, but I can't guarantee there won't be any.

ATTICUS. Don't be foolish, Heck. This is Maycomb.

HECK. I'm just uneasy, that's all.

ATTICUS. Trial'll probably begin day after tomorrow. You can keep him till then, can't you? *(Smiling.)* I don't think anybody'll begrudge me a client with times this hard.

HECK *(smiling back).* It's just that Old Sarum bunch. You know how they do when they get shinnied up.

ATTICUS. Are they drinking?

HECK. Could be. *(Worried.)* I don't see why you touched this case. You've got everything to lose.

ATTICUS *(quietly).* Do you really think so?

*(At this, SCOUT comes to the porch rail followed by DILL.)*

HECK *(taking breath, frankly).* Yes, I do, Atticus. I mean —everything.

ATTICUS *(with decision).* Heck, that boy might go to the chair, but he's not going till the truth's told.

HECK *(resigned).* Okay, Mr. Finch.

ATTICUS. And you know as well as I do what the truth is.

*(JEM, coming from the DUBOSE house, pauses as HE sees HECK and ATTICUS.)*

HECK *(withdrawn)*. I just thought I should keep you informed.

ATTICUS. And I appreciate it, Heck. Thank you.

HECK *(relaxing again)*. Sure—well, take care of yourself. *(HECK goes off.)*

ATTICUS *(after him, smiling)*. Don't worry. *(As JEM approaches.)* Well, Son?

JEM. I told her I'd work on her garden and try to make it grow back. And I said I was sorry—but I'm not. What was Heck Tate—

ATTICUS *(cutting in)*. No point in saying you're sorry if you aren't.

JEM. How about what *she* said?

ATTICUS. She's old and she's ill. *(Going back into the house.)* I have work.

JEM *(after him)*. She wants me to read to her. *(ATTICUS pauses.)* She wants me to come over every afternoon and read out loud for two hours. Atticus—do I have to?

ATTICUS. You do.

JEM *(protesting)*. Her house is so dark—creepy—shadows on the ceiling.

ATTICUS *(smiling grimly)*. That should appeal to your imagination. *(As HE goes.)* Just pretend you're inside the Radley house. *(JEM looks after ATTICUS.)*

JEM *(perplexed)*. He's sure in a peculiar mood these days. *(Turning to DILL and SCOUT.)* What's Heck want?

DILL *(dramatic)*. Death and politics!

SCOUT. Don't be silly. It was just they moved Tom Robinson to the Maycomb jail.

DILL *(to JEM)*. Your father said I could stay. He said I could take the cot in your room.

SCOUT. What are you gonna read to Mrs. Dubose?

JEM. *Ivanhoe. (Perplexed.)* Why would she want me to read aloud?

DILL. Seemed like your father wasn't surprised.

*(ATTICUS is coming back onto the porch with CAL-*
*PURNIA. HE is carrying a small folding chair and an*
*electrical extension cord with a light bulb at the end.)*

JEM *(anxiously, to DILL).* Why wouldn't he be surprised?

DILL. Ask him.

ATTICUS. Ask me what?

JEM. Nothin'.

ATTICUS. You folks'll be in bed when I come back, so I'll say good night now.

SCOUT. Where are you goin'?

ATTICUS. Out. You mind Calpurnia.

JEM. What are you doin' with the chair and the light bulb?

ATTICUS. Might have use for them. *(As HE goes.)* Look after things, Cal.

CALPURNIA. Do my best, Mr. Finch. *(ATTICUS goes off. Lights are beginning to dim.)*

SCOUT *(turning to CALPURNIA.)* Where's he goin'?

CALPURNIA *(looking after ATTICUS, a little grimly).* I could make a guess—only I won't. You get washed— all three of you. *(CALPURNIA goes back inside.)*

DILL. I really need a wash.

SCOUT. Why wouldn't she guess? *(No one has an answer.)*

JEM. Why was Atticus taking a chair and a light bulb? *(No one has an answer for this either.)* Before I go to bed, I may walk downtown for a while.

SCOUT *(lightly).* You got a case of the lookarounds? *(As the light continues to dim, JEM goes on inside.)*

DILL *(connecting. Casually).* I may come look around, too.
SCOUT *(following them off).* What are you talking about?

*(Moment of darkness, then light as MISS MAUDIE's
door is opened and she and MISS STEPHANIE come
out on porch.)*

MISS MAUDIE. Thanks for stopping by, Stephanie.
MISS STEPHANIE. Best view in town. First Atticus goes
by with a chair and an electric light. Then three chil-
dren go after him. I can't imagine where—
MISS MAUDIE *(grimly).* My guess is the jailhouse.
*(Front.)* The jail is Maycomb's only conversation piece:
its detractors say it looks like a Victorian privy.
MISS STEPHANIE *(front).* And its supporters say it gives
the town a good, solid, respectable look, and no
stranger would ever suspect that it's full of niggers.
MISS MAUDIE *(tired).* Go home, Stephanie.
MISS STEPHANIE *(as she goes).* The cake was heavenly.

*(ATTICUS has meanwhile seated himself in his chair,
opened his newspaper, and now he turns on the bulb
hanging beside him, and starts to read. The THREE
CHILDREN are coming onto the stage.)*

SCOUT *(surprised).* A light in front of the jailhouse.
JEM *(relieved).* There he is!
SCOUT. *(starting).* Well, let's—
JEM *(grabbing her).* No, Scout.
SCOUT. I just want to ask why he's sitting in front of the
jailhouse.
DILL. Maybe we shouldn't bother him right now.
SCOUT. But—

DILL. It's pretty late.

JEM. He's all right, so let's go home. I just wanted to see where he was. *(The sound of approaching cars is heard.)*

SCOUT. After all this runnin' 'round town, we might at least—

JEM. Shh—

SCOUT. He can't hear me.

JEM. No—*listen*!

DILL. It's cars. A lotta cars coming. *(The sound is getting closer, and then it stops.)*

JEM *(nervously)*. I wonder what—

DILL. So many.

JEM *(hushed, urgent)*. Get down. We'll get down 'n' watch.

*(THEY get down to watch, unseen. The stage light is quite dim now except for the small area around ATTICUS, who has meanwhile looked up at the sound. HE closes his newspaper, folds it and puts it in his lap. Then HE pushes his hat back on his head, waiting.)*

SCOUT *(a half-scared whisper)*. What's happening?

JEM *(whispering back)*. Quiet!

*(In the darkness, a GROUP of MEN come on, seen only dimly, moving slowly and deliberately toward ATTICUS. The GROUP includes MR. CUNNINGHAM and BOB EWELL; the rest of the "mob" are EXTRAS and not identifiable in the dim light; they are ALL dressed in farm clothes. THEY are facing toward ATTICUS, sullen, determined and ominous.)*

BOB EWELL. He in there, Mr. Finch?

ATTICUS. He is, and he's asleep. Don't wake him up.

MR. CUNNINGHAM. You know what we want. Step aside from the door, Mr. Finch.

ATTICUS. You can turn around and go home again, Mr. Cunningham.

MR. CUNNINGHAM. Won't do that.

ATTICUS (*pleasantly*). Might as well. Heck Tate's around somewhere.

BOB EWELL. The hell he is.

THIRD MAN. Heck's bunch's so deep in the woods, they won't get out till morning.

ATTICUS. Indeed? Why so?

THIRD MAN. Called 'em off on a snipe hunt.

BOB EWELL (*crowing*). Didn't you think o' that, Mr. Finch?

ATTICUS. Thought about it, but didn't believe it.

MR. CUNNINGHAM. Guess that changes things.

BOB EWELL. Oh, yes, it do!

ATTICUS (*getting up from his chair*). Do you really think so? (*At this, SCOUT is getting up. ATTICUS and the GROUP face each other.*)

JEM (*concerned*). He said—'Do you really think so?'

SCOUT. Means he's gonna deal with somebody. I'm gonna see this! (*SHE darts forward.*)

JEM (*after her, anxiously*). Scout! Wait! (*But SCOUT rushes up through the GROUP.*)

SCOUT (*as SHE comes*). H—ey, Atticus!

ATTICUS (*startled, afraid for her*). Scout! (*JEM and DILL are following into the circle of light.*)

JEM (*apologetic*). Couldn't hang onto her.

ATTICUS (*urgently*). Go home, Jem. Take Scout and Dill and go home. (*JEM is looking at the GROUP.*) Jem—I said, go home.

JEM *(back to ATTICUS)*. Will you be coming with us?

ATTICUS. Son, I told you—*(A FOURTH MAN grabs JEM.)*

FOURTH MAN. I'll send him home.

SCOUT. Don't you touch him!

FOURTH MAN. I'm telling you to—*(SCOUT kicks the FOURTH MAN in the shins, and HE cries out, letting go of JEM and hopping back into the GROUP.)*

ATTICUS. That'll do, Scout. Don't kick folks.

SCOUT *(indignant)*. But he—

ATTICUS. No, Scout.

SCOUT. Nobody gonna do Jem that way.

THIRD MAN. All right, Mr. Finch, *you* get 'em outa here.

BOB EWELL. Give ya fifteen seconds.

JEM. I ain't goin'.

ATTICUS. *Please*, Jem, take them and go.

JEM *(grimly determined)*. No, sir. *(The CROWD is stirring with impatience.)*

CROWD *(muttering angry)*. Had about enough—the kids are *his* worry—Can't stand around all night—come on —get 'em outa the way—let's get that nigger! *(The LAST SPEAKER is interrupted as SCOUT thinks SHE recognizes a MAN in front.)*

SCOUT. Mr. Cunningham—that you? *(Coming closer.)* Hey, Mr. Cunningham. *(MR. CUNNINGHAM does not reply. The OTHERS are watching. SCOUT is more confused.)* Don't you remember me? I'm Scout. You brought us a big bag of turnip greens, remember?

ATTICUS *(perplexed)*. Scout—

SCOUT *(struggling for recognition)*. I go to school with your boy, Walter. Well, he's your boy, ain't he? Ain't he, sir? *(MR. CUNNINGHAM is moved to a small nod. SCOUT is relieved.)* Knew he was your boy. Maybe he told you about me—because I beat him up one time.

Tell Walter "hey" for me, won't you? *(There is no reply. SHE tries harder to break through this baffling lack of response.)* My father was telling me about your entailment. He said they're bad. *(The lack of response is getting more disturbing.)* Atticus—I was just sayin' to Mr. Cunningham that entailments are bad—but I remember you said not to worry—it takes long sometimes—but you'd all ride it out together. *(SCOUT has come to a stop, looking out at the silent MEN. SHE swallows.)* What is it? Can't anybody tell me? *(A plea.)* What's the matter? *(A cry.)* Mr. Cunningham! *(Suddenly MR. CUNNINGHAM puts his hands on both of SCOUT's shoulders.)*

MR. CUNNINGHAM. Ain't nothin' the matter, little lady. An' I'll tell my boy you said "hey." *(With this, MR. CUNNINGHAM straightens up and waves his hand. With authority.)* Let's clear out of here, boys. *(There is a moment of hesitation. Firmly.)* Boys! We're goin' home! *(With this, the MEN start moving off.)*

JEM *(with hushed astonishment)*. They're goin'!

ATTICUS *(a bit astonished himself)*. Looks that way.

SCOUT *(going up to him)*. Atticus—can *we* go home now?

ATTICUS *(takes out a handkerchief with which HE wipes his face, and then blows his nose. Nodding)*. Yes. Looks like we can go home now. *(There is the sound of cars starting up and driving away. THEY look toward the sound.)*

JEM. I thought Mr. Cunningham was a friend.

ATTICUS. Still is. He just has his blind spots along with the rest of us.

JEM. But he was ready to hurt you.

ATTICUS. Because he was part of a mob. But a mob's always made up of people, and Mr. Cunningham's still a man. What you children did—you made him remember that.

*(A soft, husky voice, that of TOM ROBINSON, calls from behind, inside the jail.)*

TOM *(off, from the darkness)*. Mr. Finch? *(THEY turn toward the VOICE.)* They gone?

ATTICUS. They're gone, Tom. They won't bother you anymore.

TOM *(off)*. Thank you, Mr. Finch.

ATTICUS. We're going to have a busy time. Better get your sleep.

TOM *(wryly humorous)*. You better get some sleep, too. *(ATTICUS smiles as HE gathers his things together.*

ATTICUS. That's my intention. Good night, Tom. *(DILL has come up to ATTICUS.)*

DILL *(respectfully)*. Can I carry the chair for you, Mr. Finch? *(ATTICUS considers the request, then hands the folded chair to DILL.)*

ATTICUS. Why, thank you, Son. *(DILL is deeply pleased.)*

SCOUT *(drained)*. I want to go home. *(ATTICUS affectionately grabs JEM's shoulder with one hand and SCOUT's with the other.)*

ATTICUS. You two certainly don't mind very well.

SCOUT *(puzzled)*. Atticus—what was it you said we did to Mr. Cunningham?

ATTICUS. You made him stand in my shoes for a minute. *(With this, ATTICUS reaches up and turns out the light bulb. In the darkness ATTICUS, JEM and DILL exit. Meanwhile, the only light on the stage is a spot on MISS MAUDIE.)*

MISS MAUDIE. The next Monday, people were streaming into town like it was Saturday. Seemed like the whole county was coming for Tom Robinson's trial.

*(MISS STEPHANIE, all dressed up, is coming on.)*

MISS MAUDIE. And where are you going?
MISS STEPHANIE. To the Jitney Jungle.
MISS MAUDIE. With a hat and gloves?
MISS STEPHANIE. I might just look in at the courthouse; see what Atticus is up to.
MISS MAUDIE. Be careful he doesn't hand you a subpoena. *(With a smile.)* You seem to know so much about the case.

*(MISS STEPHANIE goes off into the group of assembling SPECTATORS. JEM, DILL and SCOUT are coming on cautiously.)*

JEM. Let's wait till the last—don't let Atticus see us. *(They keep themselves small.)*
MISS MAUDIE. When I reached the courthouse square, it was covered with picnic parties. Apparently the trial was to be a gala occasion. There was no room at the public hitching rail—mules and wagons were parked under every available tree. People were washing down biscuits and syrup with warm milk from fruit jars. In the far corner of the square, Negroes sat in the sun— very quiet. At some invisible signal, they all got up and started into the courthouse.

*(During the speech, SPECTATORS are coming on carrying folding chairs which THEY set up and sit on to*

*watch the trial. Lights are coming up. JUDGE TAYLOR has taken his place behind the bench, HECK TATE sits in the witness chair, BOB EWELL and MAYELLA are on the witness bench while ATTICUS and TOM ROBINSON are at the table. MR. GILMER is standing next to the witness. THEY're frozen. SCOUT, JEM, and DILL are coming in at the side, following REVEREND SYKES.)*

SCOUT *(with concern, SHE looks at the now set scene. To JEM.)* We're too late. There's no seats.

REVEREND SYKES. You could come with me—if you'd care to sit on the colored side of the balcony. *(THEY're nodding and going with him.)*

JEM. Gosh, yes.

SCOUT *(as THEY're taking seats with REVEREND SYKES and EXTRAS, if available. Noticing).* Trial's already started. Prosecutor's taking testimony. *(Courtroom action resumes.)*

MR. GILMER. In your own words, Mr. Tate.

HECK *(replying to MR. GILMER).* Well, I was called—

MR. GILMER *(motioning toward the AUDIENCE/JURY).* Could you say it to the jury, Mr. Tate? Who called you?

HECK *(turning to AUDIENCE/JURY).* I was fetched by Bob—by Mr. Bob Ewell yonder, one night.

MR. GILMER. What night, sir?

HECK. The night of November twenty-first. I was leaving my office to go home when B—Mr. Ewell came in, very excited he was, and said, get to his house quick, some ni—Negro'd raped his girl. *(REVEREND SYKES sighs.)*

MR. GILMER. Did you go?

HECK. Certainly. Got in the car and went out as fast as I could.

MR. GILMER. And what did you find?

HECK. Found her lying on the floor. She was pretty well beat up, but I heaved her to her feet and she washed her face in the bucket, and she said she was all right.

MR. GILMER. Go on.

HECK. I asked her who hurt her and she said it was Tom Robinson. *(JUDGE TAYLOR looks at ATTICUS expecting an objection, but ATTICUS just gives a slight shake of his head. HECK takes a breath.)* Asked her if he beat her up like that; she said, yes, he had. Asked her if he took advantage of her and she said, yes, he did. I went down to Robinson's house and brought him back. She identified him as the one, so I took him in. That's all there was to it.

MR. GILMER *(returning to his seat at the table).* Thank you.

JUDGE TAYLOR. Any questions, Atticus? *(ATTICUS turns his chair to the side and crosses his legs.)*

ATTICUS *(leaning back).* Yes. Did you call a doctor, Sheriff?

HECK. No, sir.

ATTICUS *(with a slight edge).* Why not?

HECK. It wasn't necessary, Mr. Finch. But she was mighty banged up.

ATTICUS. And you didn't—

JUDGE TAYLOR *(cutting in).* He's answered the question, Atticus. He didn't call a doctor.

ATTICUS *(smiling).* Just wanted to make sure, Judge. *(Turning to HECK.)* Sheriff, you say she was mighty banged up. In what way? Just describe her injuries, Heck.

HECK. There was already bruises comin' on her arms, and she had a black eye startin'.

ATTICUS. Which eye?

HECK. Let's see—her left.

ATTICUS. Her left facing you, or her left looking the same way you were?

HECK *(thinking about it)*. That'd make it her right. It was her right eye, Mr. Finch. I remember now, she was banged up on that side of her face. *(ATTICUS looks at TOM, then back to HECK.)*

ATTICUS *(demanding)*. Please repeat what you said.

HECK. Her right eye.

ATTICUS. No—you said she was banged up on that side of her face. Which side?

HECK. The right side.

ATTICUS. That's all, Heck. *(HECK steps down and walks over to the bench.)*

MR. GILMER *(calling)*. Robert Ewell. *(BOB EWELL hops up and comes up to the witness chair. The COURT CLERK administers the oath.)*

CLERK. Swear to tell the truth, the whole truth, and nothing but the truth?

BOB EWELL *(crowing)*. So help me God. *(MR. GILMER nods toward the chair; EWELL sits.)*

MR. GILMER. Mr. Robert Ewell?

BOB EWELL. That's m'name cap'n. *(MR. GILMER does not particularly like EWELL.)*

MR. GILMER. Are you the father of Mayella Ewell?

BOB EWELL. Well, if I ain't I can't do anything about it now. Her ma's dead.

JUDGE TAYLOR. Are you the father of Mayella Ewell?

BOB EWELL *(cowed)*. Yes, sir.

JUDGE TAYLOR. Get this straight. There will be no audibly obscene speculations on any subject from anybody

in this courtroom. Do you understand? *(EWELL nods.)*
All right, Mr. Gilmer.

MR. GILMER. Thank you, sir. Mr. Ewell, tell us what
happened on the evening of November twenty-first.

BOB EWELL. I was comin' in from the woods with a
load o' kindlin' and just as I got to the fence, I heard
Mayella screamin' like a stuck hog inside the house.

MR. GILMER. What time was it, Mr. Ewell?

BOB EWELL. Just 'fore sundown. Well, I was sayin',
Mayella was screamin' fit to beat Jesus! *(The JUDGE
clears his throat, irritated, and BOB EWELL hesitates.)*

MR. GILMER *(prodding).* Yes? She was screaming?

BOB EWELL. She was raising this holy racket so I
dropped m' load and run as fast as I could up to the
window—and I seen—I seen—*(HE gets up and points
angrily at TOM ROBINSON. With all his strength.) I
seen that black nigger yonder ruttin on my Mayella!
(There is a gasp from the SPECTATORS. MR. GILMER
is going up to the bench, where HE speaks quietly to
the JUDGE. REVEREND SYKES leans across to JEM.)*

REVEREND SYKES. Mr. Jem. Take Miss Scout home.
Mr. Jem, you hear me?

JEM *(turning to her).* Scout—go home. Dill, you 'n'
Scout go home.

SCOUT. You can't make me.

JEM *(to REVEREND SYKES).* I think it's okay, Reverend.
She doesn't understand.

SCOUT. I most certainly do.

REVEREND SYKES *(disturbed).* This ain't fit for Miss
Scout—or you boys, either. *(REVEREND SYKES and
the OTHER SPECTATORS, talking excitedly to each
other, are interrupted by JUDGE TAYLOR, who is banging his gavel for attention.)*

JUDGE TAYLOR. Quiet! There has been a request that this courtroom be cleared of spectators, or at least of women and children—a request that for the time being will be denied. People generally see what they look for, and hear what they listen for. And they have the right to make whatever decisions they consider best for their children. You may feel there's something here to be learned. Or you may decide you do not wish to face this problem. It's up to you to make the decision. I suggest you do it right now. I'm interrupting this trial for a ten-minute recess. *(The JUDGE bangs the gavel and rises. As HE does—)*

### LIGHTS DIM OUT

### END OF ACT ONE

# ACT TWO

SCENE: *Revealed is the trial scene with EVERYONE back in place after the short recess declared by JUDGE TAYLOR. BOB EWELL is in the witness stand, MR. GILMER stands near him waiting, ATTICUS sits at his table with TOM ROBINSON, and the SPECTATORS are seated, as before. The JURY is considered to be in the audience and when addressed, the SPEAKER speaks to the AUDIENCE.*

JUDGE TAYLOR *(looking about; dryly).* I see we still have a few with us. Well, let's get on. *(HE raps casually with his gavel and turns to EWELL.)* Mr. Ewell, you will keep your testimony within the confines of Christian English usage, if that's possible. *(Nods.)* Proceed, Mr. Gilmer.

MR. GILMER *(uneasily).* Where were we? We were—

JUDGE TAYLOR *(to the point).* Mr. Ewell, did you see the defendant having sexual intercourse with your daughter?

BOB EWELL. Yes, I did.

MR. GILMER *(to the JUDGE).* Thank you, sir. *(To EWELL.)* You said you were at the window?

BOB EWELL. Yes, sir.

MR. GILMER. Did you have a clear view of the room?

BOB EWELL. Yes, sir.

MR. GILMER. How did the room look?

BOB EWELL. All slung about, like there was a fight.

MR. GILMER. What did you do when you saw the defendant?

BOB EWELL. I run around the house to get in, but he run out the front door just ahead of me. I sawed who he was, but I was too distracted about Mayella to run after him. Mayella was in there squallin', so I run in the house.

MR. GILMER. Then what did you do?

BOB EWELL. I run for Heck Tate quick as I could. I knowed who it was all right, passed the house every day, lived down yonder in that nigger-nest. *(Turning to the JUDGE.)* Jedge, I've asked this county for fifteen years to clean out that nest down yonder. They're dangerous to live around. *(Speaking as a "put-upon" citizen.)* 'Sides devaluin' my property.

MR. GILMER *(wincing; hurriedly)*. That's all. Thank you. Mr. Ewell.

*(Well-satisfied with himself, EWELL hops down, smiling as HE goes. HE bumps into ATTICUS, who is approaching. There is a stir of amusement from the SPECTATORS, which EWELL construes as approval.)*

ATTICUS *(meanwhile; genially)*. Just a minute, sir. Could I ask you a question or two? *(EWELL darts a glance at the JUDGE, who nods his head toward the witness chair.)*

BOB EWELL *(going back)*. Sure—go ahead.

ATTICUS. Thank you, Mr. Ewell. Folks were doing a lot of running that night. Let's see, you say you ran to the house, you ran to the window, you ran inside, you ran for Mr. Tate. Did you, during all this running, run for a doctor?

BOB EWELL. Wadn't no need to.

ATTICUS. Didn't you think the nature of your daughter's injuries warranted immediate medical attention?

BOB EWELL. Never called a doctor in my life. If I had, would've cost me five dollars. That all the questions?

ATTICUS. Not quite. Mr. Ewell, you heard the sheriff's testimony, didn't you?

BOB EWELL (*deciding it is safe to answer*). Yes.

ATTICUS. Do you agree with his description of Mayella's injuries? Her right eye blackened, that she was beaten around the—

BOB EWELL. Yeah. I hold with everything Tate said.

ATTICUS. He said her right eye was blackened.

BOB EWELL. I holds with Tate.

ATTICUS. Mr. Ewell, can you read and write?

MR. GILMER. Objection. Can't see what witness's literacy has to do with the case, irrelevant 'n' immaterial.

ATTICUS (*quickly*). Judge, if you'll allow the question, plus another one, you'll soon see.

JUDGE TAYLOR. All right. But make sure we see, Atticus. (*To MR. GILMER.*) Overruled.

ATTICUS (*to EWELL*). Will you write your name and show us?

BOB EWELL. I most positively will. How do you think I sign my relief checks? (*There is an amused stir among the SPECTATORS. ATTICUS is taking an envelope from his pocket and then unscrewing his fountain pen.*)

SCOUT (*while this is happening; a worried whisper*). Jem —do you think Atticus knows what he's doin'?

JEM (*uncertainly*). *Seems* like he knows.

SCOUT. Far back as I c'n remember, he said never, never, never ask a question on cross-examination unless you already know the answer.

JEM *(he remembers, too)*. 'Cause you might get an answer that'll wreck your case.

SCOUT *(watching again; nervously)*. Looks to me like he's gone frog-sticking without a light.

*(ATTICUS has presented the envelope to BOB EWELL, shaken the fountain pen and given him that, too.)*

ATTICUS. Would you write your name for us? Clearly now, so the jury can see you do it. *(With a flourish, EWELL finishes writing his name.)*

MR. GILMER *(curiously)*. What's so interestin'?

JUDGE TAYLOR. He's left-handed.

ATTICUS *(nodding)*. That's it.

BOB EWELL *(outraged)*. What's my bein' left-handed have to do with it? *(To JUDGE TAYLOR.)* He's tryin' to take advantage of me. Tricking lawyers like Atticus Finch take advantage of me all the time with their tricking ways. But it don't change what I saw, and I'll say it again—I saw that nigger—

ATTICUS. That's all, Mr. Ewell. *(The furious LITTLE MAN is stalking back to his seat.)*

JEM *(meanwhile)*. I think we've got him.

SCOUT. Don't count your chickens.

DILL *(hushed, eager)*. Her *right* eye was blacked so it had to be someone left-handed.

SCOUT *(hushed in reply)*. Maybe Tom Robinson's left-handed.

MR. GILMER *(calling)*. Mayella Violet Ewell. *(As MAY-ELLA approaches, the COURT CLERK administers the oath.)*

CLERK. Swear to tell the truth, the whole truth and nothing but the truth.

MAYELLA *(nodding softly)*. Yes. *(MAYELLA sits.)*

MR. GILMER. Please tell the jury in your own words what happened on the evening of November twenty-first. *(MAYELLA does not reply.)* Where were you at dusk on that evening?

MAYELLA. On the porch.

MR. GILMER *(trying to prod her along.)* What were you doing on the porch? *(MAYELLA hesitates.)*

JUDGE TAYLOR. Just tell us what happened. You can do that, can't you? *(MAYELLA does not reply.)* What are you scared of? *(MAYELLA whispers something to him from behind her hand.)* What was that?

MAYELLA *(pointing to ATTICUS)*. Him. Don't want him doin' me like he done Papa, makin' him out left-handed.

JUDGE TAYLOR *(perplexed)*. How old are you?

MAYELLA. Nineteen-and-a-half.

JUDGE TAYLOR. I see. Well, Mr. Finch has no idea of scaring you, and if he did, I'm here to stop him. Now sit up straight and tell us what happened. *(MAYELLA takes a breath, and starts nervously.)*

MAYELLA. Well—I was on the porch and—he came along and, you see, there was this old chiffarobe in the yard Papa'd brought in to chop up for kindlin'. Papa told me to do it while he was off in the woods, but I wasn't feelin' strong enough then, so he came by—

MR. GILMER. Who is 'he'?

MAYELLA. That'n yonder. Robinson.

MR. GILMER. Then what happened?

MAYELLA. I said, 'Come here, boy, and bust up this chiffarobe for me, I gotta nickel for you.' So he came in the yard an' I went in the house to get him the nickel. An' 'fore I knew it, he was on me. He got me 'round the neck. I fought, but he hit me agin and agin.

MR. GILMER *(as MAYELLA collects herself)*. Go on.

MAYELLA. An' he took advantage of me.

MR. GILMER. Did you scream and fight back?

MAYELLA. Kicked and hollered loud as I could.

MR. GILMER. Then what happened?

MAYELLA. Don't remember too good, but Papa come in the room and was hollerin' who done it? Then I sorta fainted, an' the next thing I knew Mr. Tate was helpin' me over to the water bucket.

MR. GILMER. You fought Robinson hard as you could —tooth and nail?

MAYELLA. I positively did.

MR. GILMER. You are positive he took full advantage of you?

MAYELLA *(holding back a sob)*. I already told ya. He done what he was after.

MR. GILMER. That's all for now. But stay here. I expect big, bad Mr. Finch has some questions.

JUDGE TAYLOR *(primly)*. State will not prejudice the witness against counsel for the defense.

*(ATTICUS, smiling, has risen. HE opens his coat, hooks his thumbs in his vest and without looking directly at MAYELLA, speaks casually to her.)*

ATTICUS. Miss Mayella, I won't try to scare you for a while, not yet. Let's get acquainted. How old are you?

MAYELLA. Said I was nineteen, said it to the judge yonder.

ATTICUS. You'll have to bear with me, Miss Mayella. I can't remember as well as I used to. I might ask you things you've already said before, but you'll give me an answer, won't you? Good.

MAYELLA. Won't answer a word as long as you keep on mockin' me.

ATTICUS *(startled)*. Ma'am?

MAYELLA. Long as you call me 'ma'am' and say 'Miss Mayella.' *(To JUDGE TAYLOR.)* I don't have to take his sass.

JUDGE TAYLOR. That's just Mr. Finch's way. We've done business in this court for years and Mr. Finch is always courteous. Atticus, let's get on—and let the record show that the witness has not been sassed.

ATTICUS. How many sisters and brothers have you?

MAYELLA. Seb'm.

ATTICUS. You the oldest?

MAYELLA. Yes.

ATTICUS. How long has your mother been dead?

MAYELLA. Don't know. Long time.

ATTICUS. How long did you go to school?

MAYELLA. Two year—three year—dunno.

ATTICUS. Miss Mayella, a nineteen-year-old girl must have friends. Who are your friends?

MAYELLA *(puzzled)*. Friends?

ATTICUS. Don't you know anyone near your age? Boys —girls—just ordinary friends?

MAYELLA *(angry)*. You makin' fun o' me again, Mr. Finch?

ATTICUS. Do you love your father, Miss Mayella?

MAYELLA. Love him, whatcha mean?

ATTICUS. Is he good to you, is he easy to get along with?

MAYELLA. He does toll'able 'cept when—

ATTICUS. Except when?

MAYELLA. I said he does toll'able.

ATTICUS *(gently)*. Except when he's drinking? *(The question is asked so gently that in spite of herself, MAYELLA nods.)* When he's riled—has he ever beaten you? *(MAYELLA looks around, startled.)*

JUDGE TAYLOR. Answer the question, Miss Mayella.

MAYELLA. My paw's never touched a hair o' my head—

ATTICUS *(considers her a moment)*. We've had a good visit, Miss Mayella. Now we'd better get to the case. You say you asked Tom Robinson to come chop up a—what was it?

MAYELLA. A chiffarobe, a old dresser.

ATTICUS. Was Tom Robinson well known to you?

MAYELLA. Whaddya mean?

ATTICUS. Did you know who he was, where he lived?

MAYELLA *(nodding)*. I knowed who he was. He passed the house every day.

ATTICUS *(turning away; casually)*. Was this the first time you asked him to come inside the fence? *(MAYELLA jumps, looking about nervously.)* Was this—

MAYELLA. Yes, it was.

ATTICUS. Didn't you ever ask him to come inside the fence before?

MAYELLA *(ready now)*. I did not. I certainly did not.

ATTICUS *(serenely)*. You never asked him to do odd jobs for you before?

MAYELLA *(conceding)*. I mighta. There was several niggers around.

ATTICUS. Can you remember any other occasions?

MAYELLA. No.

ATTICUS (*firmly*). All right, now to what happened. You said Tom Robinson got you around the neck—is that right?

MAYELLA. Yes.

ATTICUS. You say—'he caught me and choked me and took advantage of me'—is that right?

MAYELLA. That's what I said.

ATTICUS. Do you remember him beating you about the face? (*MAYELLA hesitates.*) You're sure enough he choked you. All this time you were fighting back, remember? You kicked and hollered. Do you remember him beating you about the face? (*MAYELLA is looking about, uncertain how to reply.*) It's an easy question, Miss Mayella, so I'll try again. Do you remember him beating you about the face?

MAYELLA. No, I don't recollect if he hit me. I mean, yes, I do, he hit me.

ATTICUS. Was your last sentence your answer?

MAYELLA. Yes, he hit—I just don't remember—it all happened so quick!

JUDGE TAYLOR. Don't you cry, young woman.

ATTICUS. Let her cry, if she wants to, Judge. We've got all the time in the world.

MAYELLA (*sniffing wrathfully*). Get me up here an' mock me, will you? I'll answer any questions you got.

ATTICUS. That's fine. There's only a few more. Will you identify the man who attacked you?

MAYELLA. I will. That's him right yonder.

ATTICUS. Tom, stand up. Let Miss Mayella have a good look at you. Is this the man, Miss Mayella? (*TOM stands. HE is a powerful young man, but his left hand is curled up and held to his chest.*)

JEM *(hushed)*. Scout—Reverend—his left hand! He's crippled!

REVEREND SYKES *(whispering)*. Caught in a cotton gin when he was a boy. Tore all the muscles loose.

ATTICUS. Is this the man who attacked you?

MAYELLA. It most certainly is.

ATTICUS *(hard)*. How?

MAYELLA *(raging)*. I don't know how, but he did. I said it all happened so fast I—

ATTICUS. Let's consider calmly.

MR. GILMER. Objection. He's browbeating the witness.

JUDGE TAYLOR. Oh, sit down, Horace.

ATTICUS. Miss Mayella, you've testified the defendant choked and beat you. You didn't say he sneaked up behind you and knocked you cold. Do you wish to reconsider any of your testimony?

MAYELLA. You want me to say something that didn't happen?

ATTICUS. No, ma'am, I want you to say something that did happen.

MAYELLA. I already told ya.

ATTICUS. He hit you? He blackened your right eye with his right fist?

MAYELLA *(seeing the point)*. I ducked and it—it glanced. That's what it did. I ducked and it glanced off.

ATTICUS. You're a strong girl. Why didn't you run?

MAYELLA. Tried to—

ATTICUS. And you were screaming all the time?

MAYELLA. I certainly was.

ATTICUS. Why didn't the other children hear you? Where were they? *(MAYELLA makes no reply.)* Why didn't your screams make them come running? *(MAYELLA makes no reply)*. Or didn't you scream until you saw your father in the window? You didn't scream till then, did you? *(MAYELLA makes no reply.)* Did you scream at your father instead of Tom Robinson? Is that it? *(MAY-ELLA makes no reply.)* Who beat you up? Tom Robinson or your father? *(MAYELLA makes no reply.)* Miss Mayella—what did your father really see in that window? *(MAYELLA covers her mouth with her hands.)* Why don't you tell the truth, child—didn't Bob Ewell beat you up? *(With this, ATTICUS turns away, and lets out a breath. HE looks a little as though his stomach hurts. MAYELLA's face is a mixture of terror and fury.)*

MAYELLA *(gasping a quick breath and calling out).* I—I got somethin' to say. *(ATTICUS walks back and sits wearily at his table.)*

ATTICUS *(with compassion).* Do you want to tell us what happened?

MAYELLA. I got somethin' to say an' then I ain't gonna say no more. That nigger yonder took advantage of me an' if you fine fancy gentlemen don't wanta do nothin' about it then you're all yellow stinkin' cowards, stinkin' cowards, the lot of you. Your fancy airs don't come to nothin'—your ma'amin' and Miss Mayellarin' don't come to nothin', Mr. Finch. *(MAYELLA covers her face with her hands to hold back her sobs.)*

MR. GILMER. That's all. *(Helping her out of the witness chair.)* You can step down now. *(As MAYELLA continues on to the bench to sit with her FATHER, MR. GILMER turns to JUDGE TAYLOR.)* Sir—the State rests.

JUDGE TAYLOR. Shall we try to wind up this afternoon? How about it, Atticus?

ATTICUS. I think we can.

JUDGE TAYLOR. How many witnesses you got?

ATTICUS. One.

JUDGE TAYLOR. Well, call him.

ATTICUS *(rising)*. I call Tom Robinson.

*(TOM rises and walks toward the witness chair. The COURT CLERK holds out the Bible to him. TOM cannot put his crippled left hand on the Bible, so he touches it with his right.)*

TOM. Sorry, sir.

JUDGE TAYLOR. That's all right, Tom.

CLERK. Do you swear the evidence you're about to give is the truth, the whole truth, and nothing but the truth?

TOM *(nodding)*. I swear. *(TOM is motioned into the witness chair and HE sits quietly and, naturally, afraid.)*

ATTICUS. You're Tom Robinson, twenty-five years of age, married with three children, and you've been in trouble with the law once before. A thirty-day sentence for disorderly conduct. What did that consist of?

TOM. Got in a fight with another man. He tried to cut me. But it wasn't much. Not enough to hurt.

ATTICUS. You were both convicted?

TOM *(nodding)*. I had to serve 'cause I couldn't pay the fine. The other fellow paid his'n.

ATTICUS. Were you acquainted with Mayella Violet Ewell?

TOM. Yes, sir. I had to pass her place goin' to and from the field every day.

ATTICUS. Whose field?

TOM. I work for Mr. Link Deas.

ATTICUS. You pass the Ewell place to get to work. Is there any other way to go?

TOM. No, sir, none's I know of.

ATTICUS. Tom, did she ever speak to you?

TOM. Why, yes, sir. I'd tip m'hat when I'd go by and one day she asked me to come inside the fence and bust up a chiffarobe.

ATTICUS. When did she ask you to chop up the—the chiffarobe?

TOM. Mr. Finch, it was way last spring. After I broke it up she said, 'I reckon I'll hafta give you a nickel, won't I?' an' I said, 'No, ma'am, there ain't no charge.' Then I went home. That was way over a year ago.

ATTICUS. Did you ever go on the place again?

TOM. Yes, sir.

ATTICUS. When?

TOM. I went lots of times. *(There is a murmur among the SPECTATORS, and JUDGE TAYLOR raps his gavel without comment.)*

ATTICUS. Under what circumstances? *(TOM does not quite understand.)* Why did you go inside the fence lots of times?

TOM. She'd call me in. Seemed like every time I passed by yonder, she'd have somethin' for me to do— choppin' kindlin', totin' water for her.

ATTICUS. Were you paid for your services?

TOM. No, sir, not after she offered me a nickel the first time. But I was glad to do it. Mr. Ewell didn't seem to help her none, and neither did the chillun, and I knowed she didn't have no nickels to spare.

ATTICUS. Where were the other children?

TOM. They were always around, all over the place.

ATTICUS. Would Miss Mayella talk to you?

TOM. Yes, sir, she talked to me.

ATTICUS. Did you ever—at any time—go on the Ewell property—did you ever set foot on the Ewell property without an express invitation from one of them?

TOM. No, sir, Mr. Finch, I never did. I wouldn't do that, sir.

ATTICUS. Tom, what happened to you on the evening of November twenty-first? *(The SPECTATORS draw in a collective breath and lean forward.)*

TOM. Mr. Finch, I was goin' home as usual that evenin', and when I passed the Ewell place, Miss Mayella were on the porch, like she said she were. It seemed real quiet like, an' I didn't quite know why. She called to me to come there and help her a minute. Well, I went inside the fence an' looked for some kindlin' to work on, but I didn't see none, and she says, 'Naw, I got somethin' for you to do in the house. Th' old door's off its hinges.' I said, 'You got a screwdriver, Miss Mayella?' She said she had. Well, I went up the steps and she motioned for me to come inside. *(Taking a breath.)* I went in an' looked at the door. I said, 'Miss Mayella, this door look all right.' Those hinges was all right. Then she shet the door. Mr. Finch, I was wonderin' why it was so quiet like, 'n' it come to me that there weren't a chile on the place, not one of 'em, an' I said, 'Miss Mayella, where the chillun?' *(TOM pauses to run his hand over his face.)*

ATTICUS *(quietly)*. Go on, Tom.

TOM. I say where the chillun, an' she says—she was laughin' sort of—she says they all gone to town to get ice creams. She says, 'Took me a slap year to save seb'm nickels, but I done it. They all gone to town.' *(Intensely uncomfortable and shifting in his seat, TOM stops.)*

ATTICUS. Tom, what did you say then?

TOM *(taking a breath)*. I said somethin' like, 'Why, Miss Mayella, that's right smart o' you to treat 'em.' An' she

said, 'You think so?' I don't think she understood what
I was thinkin'—I meant it was smart of her to save like
that, an' nice of her to treat 'em.

ATTICUS. I understand. Go on.

TOM. I said I best be goin', I couldn't do nothin' for her,
an' she says oh yes I could, an' I ask her what, an' she
says to just step on that chair yonder an' git that box
down from on top of the chiffarobe.

ATTICUS. Not the same one you busted up?

TOM (smiling). No, sir, another one. Most as tall as the
room. So I done what she told me, an' I was just
reachin' when she—she grabbed me round the legs, Mr.
Finch, She scared me so bad I hopped down an' turned
the chair over—that was the only thing, only furniture
'sturbed in that room, Mr. Finch, when I left it. I swear
'fore God.

ATTICUS. What happened after you turned the chair over?
(TOM has come to a stop, looking about the room nervously.) Tom, you've sworn to tell the whole truth. (TOM
still hesitates.) What happened after that?

JUDGE TAYLOR. Answer the question.

TOM. When I got down offa that chair, she sorta—jumped
at me.

ATTICUS. Jumped? Violently?

TOM. No, sir, she—she hugged me. She hugged me. She
hugged me round the waist. (There's a growing murmur as the SPECTATORS react to each other at this. It
is cut short by JUDGE TAYLOR's gavel.)

ATTICUS. Tom—what did she do then?

TOM (swallowing hard). She reached up and kissed me
'side of th' face. She says she never kissed a grown
man before and she might as well start with a nigger.
She say, 'Kiss me back, nigger.' I say, 'Miss Mayella,

lemme outa here,' an' I tried to run, but she got her back to the door an' I'da had to push her. I didn't wanta harm her, Mr. Finch, an' I say 'lemme pass,' but just when I say it, Mr. Ewell yonder hollered through th' window.

ATTICUS. What did he say?

TOM. Somethin' not fittin' to say—not fittin' for these folks 'n' chillun to hear.

ATTICUS. Tom you *must* tell the jury what he said.

TOM *(shutting his eyes)*. He says, 'You goddamn whore, I'll kill ya!'

ATTICUS. Then what happened?

TOM *(opening his eyes again; unhappily)*. I was runnin' so fast, Mr. Finch, I didn't know what happened.

ATTICUS. Tom, did you attack Mayella Ewell?

TOM. I did not, sir.

ATTICUS. Did you harm her in any way?

TOM. I did not.

ATTICUS. Did you resist her advances?

TOM. Mr. Finch, I tried to 'thout bein' ugly to her. I didn't wanta be ugly. I didn't wanta push her or nothin'.

ATTICUS. Let's go back to Mr. Ewell. Who was he talking to?

TOM. He were talkin' and lookin' at Miss Mayella.

ATTICUS. Then you ran.

TOM. I sure did.

ATTICUS. Why did you run?

TOM. I was scared, sir.

ATTICUS. Why were you scared?

TOM. Mr. Finch, if you was a nigger like me, you'd be scared, too.

*(ATTICUS nods agreement with this, turns to MR. GIL-MER as though saying, 'Your witness,' and goes back to his chair. MR. GILMER is rising and moving toward TOM. As this happens, a VOICE calls from the SPEC-TATORS, or from off.)*

VOICE *(off)*. I want the whole lot of you to know one thing right now. Tom Robinson's worked for me eight years an' I ain't had a speck o' trouble outa him. Not a speck.

JUDGE TAYLOR *(rapping angrily with his gavel)*. That's enough, Link Deas. If you have anything to say, you can say it under oath and at the proper time. *(To the JURY.)* You're to disregard the remark from Link Deas. *(Turning to MR. GILMER.)* Go ahead, Mr. Gilmer.

MR. GILMER. You were given thirty days for disorderly conduct, Robinson?

TOM. Yes, suh.

MR. GILMER. What'd the nigger look like when you got through with him?

TOM. He beat me, Mr. Gilmer.

MR. GILMER. Yes, but you were convicted, weren't you?

ATTICUS *(from his chair)*. It was a misdemeanor and it's in the record, Judge.

JUDGE TAYLOR. Witness'll answer, though.

TOM. Yes, sir. I got thirty days. *(MR. GILMER looks significantly at the AUDIENCE/JURY then turns back to TOM.)*

MR. GILMER. You're pretty good at busting up chiffa-robes and kindling with one hand, aren't you?

TOM. Yes, sir. I reckon so.

MR. GILMER. Strong enough to choke the breath out of a woman.

TOM. I never done that, sir.

MR. GILMER. But you're strong enough?

TOM. I reckon so, sir.

MR. GILMER. Had your eye on her for a long time, hadn't you, boy?

TOM. No, sir. I never looked at her.

MR. GILMER. Then you were mighty polite to do all that chopping and hauling for her, weren't you, boy?

TOM. I was just tryin' to help out, sir.

MR. GILMER. That was mighty generous of you. Why were you so anxious to do that woman's chores?

TOM *(hesitating)*. Looked like she didn't have nobody to help her.

MR. GILMER. With Mr. Ewell and seven children on the place, boy?

TOM. Well, I says it looked like they never help her none.

MR. GILMER. You did all this chopping and work for sheer goodness, boy?

TOM. Just tried to help her.

MR. GILMER. You're a mighty good fellow, it seems— did all this for not one penny.

TOM. Yes, sir. I felt right sorry for her. She seemed to try more'n the rest of 'em.

MR. GILMER *(got him)*. *You* felt sorry for *her*! You felt *sorry* for her! *(The SPECTATORS are shifting uncomfortably at this. To the JURY.)* He felt sorry for her. *(Turning back to TOM.)* Now you went by the house as usual last November twenty-first and she asked you to come in and bust up the chiffarobe?

TOM. No, sir.

MR. GILMER. Do you deny you went by the house?

TOM. No, sir.

MR. GILMER. She says she asked you to bust up the chiffarobe. Is that right?

TOM. No, sir, it ain't.

MR. GILMER *(his tone is dangerous)*. You say she's lying, boy? *(ATTICUS is rising to protest, but TOM handles the question.)*

TOM. I don't say she's lying, Mr. Gilmer. I say she's mistaken in her mind. *(ATTICUS sits again.)*

MR. GILMER *(his tone rougher)*. Tell me, boy. Why did you run away?

TOM. I was scared, sir.

MR. GILMER. If you had a clear conscience, boy, why were you scared?

TOM. Like I says before, it weren't safe for any nigger to be in a—fix like that.

MR. GILMER *(sarcastically)*. But you weren't in a fix. You testified you were resisting her advances. Were you scared she might hurt you—a big buck like you?

TOM. No, sir. I was scared I'd be in court, just like I am now.

MR. GILMER *(his voice rising)*. Scared you'd have to face up to what you did?

TOM. No, sir. Scared I'd have to face up to what I didn't do.

MR. GILMER. You bein' impudent to me, boy?

TOM. I didn't go to be.

MR. GILMER *(walking away)*. No more questions.

JUDGE TAYLOR. You can step down, Mr. Robinson.

*(As TOM finds his way back to his chair, the light on the court scene dims as a spot of light comes up DR into which DILL comes, followed by SCOUT. DILL is upset.)*

SCOUT. 'smatter with you?

DILL *(with an effort)*. I'm okay.

SCOUT. The heat got you? Ain't you feeling good?

DILL *(getting himself in hand)*. Said I was okay.

SCOUT. Then why'd you run out?

DILL *(covering)*. It's just I'm beginning to understand some things. Like why Boo Radley stays shut up in his house—it's because he wants to stay inside.

SCOUT. That don't make any sense.

DILL. Maybe he found out the way people can go outa their way to despise each other. *(Bursting out of him.)* Why'd Mr. Gilmer have to do Tom Robinson that-away? Why'd he talk so hateful?

SCOUT. Dill, that's his job.

DILL. But he didn't have to sneer, and call him 'boy.'

SCOUT. That's just Mr. Gilmer's way. They do all defendants that way, most lawyers, I mean.

DILL. Mr. Finch doesn't.

SCOUT. He's not an example, Dill, he's—well, the same in the courtroom as he is at home—or on the street. *(DILL nods patiently, making SCOUT speak with a slight edge.)* Might be better if Atticus was a little more —if he was—

DILL *(exasperated)*. Don't you realize yet—your father's not a run-of-the-mill man.

SCOUT *(dubiously)*. Most people—

DILL *(cutting in with a snort)*. Whatta you care about most people? Can't you realize—

SCOUT *(not liking DILL's superiority)*. If you've got over your cryin' fit, I guess I can take you back in.

DILL. Wasn't a cryin' fit. *(Going to her.)* Just didn't like the way Mr. Gilmer—*(SCOUT and DILL return to their seats.)*

SCOUT *(with whispered superiority)*. That's because you don't understand about the law.

*(The light is coming up on the trial area with EVERY-ONE seated except ATTICUS, who stands by his table. SCOUT punches JEM for attention.)*

SCOUT. His speech to the jury? *(JEM nods.)* How long's he been at it?

JEM. Just finished going over the evidence. An', Scout— we're gonna win! I don't see how we can't!

DILL *(suspiciously)*. Did that Mr. Gilmer—

JEM. Nothin' new. Just the usual. Hush now.

ATTICUS *(has paused by the table, unbuttoning his vest and collar, and loosening his tie. Looking up to the JUDGE)*. With the court's permission? *(JUDGE TAY-LOR nods, and ATTICUS takes off his coat and vest and puts them on his chair.)*

JEM *(startled)*. Never saw him do that before.

SCOUT *(equally impressed)*. Me either. *(They are ALL leaning forward. ATTICUS looks directly out to the AU-DIENCE/JURY.)*

ATTICUS *(still at his table)*. Gentlemen, this case is not a difficult one, it requires no minute sifting of compli-cated facts. This case is as simple as black and white. *(ATTICUS moves slowly to the front of the stage.)* The State has not produced one iota of evidence that the crime Tom Robinson is charged with ever took place. It has relied instead upon the testimony of two witnes-ses—witnesses whose testimony has not only been called into serious question on cross-examination, but has been flatly contradicted by the defendant. *(ATTI-CUS looks back at MAYELLA.)* I have nothing but pity in my heart for the chief witness for the state. But my pity does not extend to her putting a man's life at stake. And this is what she's done—done it in an effort to get rid of *her* guilt! I say guilt, because it was guilt that motivated her. She committed no crime, but she broke a rigid code of our society, a code so severe that whoever breaks it is hounded from our midst as unfit to live with. She's the victim of cruel poverty and ignorance, but she knew full well the enormity of her offense and she persisted in it. *(ATTICUS pauses and takes a breath.)* She persisted and her subsequent reaction is something every child has done—she tried to put the evidence of her offense away, out of sight. What was the evidence? Not a stolen toy to be hidden. The evidence that must be destroyed is Tom Robinson, a human being. Tom Robinson, a daily reminder of what she did. What did she do? She tempted a Negro. She did something that in our society is unspeakable. She's white and she tempted a Negro. Not an old uncle, but a strong, young black man. No code mattered to her before she broke it—but it came crashing down on her afterwards! Her father saw what happened. And what did he do? *(ATTICUS looks at EWELL.)* There is circumstantial evidence to the effect that Mayella Ewell was beaten savagely by someone who led almost exclusively with his left hand. *(EWELL rises, fists clenched.)*

BOB EWELL *(furious)*. Damn you ta—*(JUDGE TAYLOR raps sharply for order, and HECK TATE motions EWELL down while ATTICUS watches, unimpressed.)*

ATTICUS. Then Mr. Ewell swore out a warrant, no doubt signing it with his left hand, and Tom Robinson now sits before you, having taken the oath with the only good hand he possesses—his right hand!

BOB EWELL *(back on his feet; raging).* You trickin' lyin'—
JUDGE TAYLOR *(rapping hard; angry).* Shut your mouth, sir, or you'll be fined for contempt! *(EWELL is forced back into his seat by HECK TATE.)*
ATTICUS. So a quiet, respectable Negro man who had the unmitigated temerity to feel sorry for a white woman is on trial for his life. He's had to put his word against his two white accusers. I need not remind you of *their* conduct here in court—their cynical confidence that you gentlemen would go along with them on the assumption—the evil assumption—that *all* Negroes lie, that *all* Negroes are basically immoral, an assumption one associates with minds of their caliber. However, you know the truth—and the truth is, *some* Negroes lie, and *some* Negro men are not to be trusted around women—black or white. And so with some white men. This is a truth that applies to the entire human race, and to no particular race. *(ATTICUS pauses to clean his glasses with his handkerchief, speaking in a casual, lower key as he does so.)* In this year of grace, 1935, we're beginning to hear more and more references to Thomas Jefferson's phrase about all men being created equal. But we know that all men are *not* created equal —in the sense that some men are smarter than others, some have more opportunity because they're born with it, some men make more money, some ladies make better cakes, some people are born gifted beyond the normal scope— *(ATTICUS puts his glasses back on. Speaking directly to the AUDIENCE/JURY, he comes all the way D to the front of the stage. His manner has changed and HE is speaking with controlled passion.)* But there's one way in which all men *are* created equal. There's one human institution that makes the pauper the equal of a Rocke-

feller, the stupid man the equal to an Einstein. That institution, gentlemen, is a court of law. In our courts—all men are created equal. *(ATTICUS looks out at the AUDIENCE/JURY for a moment and then continues, totally committed.)* I'm no idealist to believe so firmly in the integrity of our courts and in the jury system—that's no ideal to me, it is a living, working reality. But a court is only as sound as its jury, and a jury is only as sound as the men who make it up. *(ATTICUS pauses to take a breath.)* I'm confident that you gentlemen will review without passion the evidence you've heard, come to a decision, and restore this defendant to his family. In the name of God, do your duty! *(ATTICUS continues to look out front for a moment, then turns, walks back, and sits at the table with TOM ROBINSON. Nothing else happens on the stage until ATTICUS is seated. Then SCOUT reaches across and punches JEM.)*

SCOUT. Did he say somethin' else? As he was walkin' back?

JEM. I think he said—'In the name of God, believe him!' *(DILL tugs at SCOUT and JEM.)*

DILL *(pointing)* Looka yonder!

*(CALPURNIA, carefully dressed, is coming shyly into the trial area. SHE pauses, waiting for recognition.)*

JUDGE TAYLOR *(becoming aware of her)*. It's Calpurnia, isn't it?

CALPURNIA. Yes, sir. Could I speak with Mr. Finch, please, sir? It hasn't got anything to do with—with the trial.

JUDGE TAYLOR *(nodding)*. Of course. *(ATTICUS is crossing over to her.)*

ATTICUS *(concerned)*. What is it, Cal? *(CALPURNIA is whispering to him quickly, and ATTICUS turns to JUDGE TAYLOR.)* Judge—she says my children are missing, haven't turned up since noon. I—could you—

MISS STEPHANIE *(calling)*. They're up there, Atticus— *(Nodding.)* Yonder.

ATTICUS *(calling)*. Jem—Scout—come down. Meet me outside. *(ATTICUS crosses to JUDGE TAYLOR and whispers something. The JUDGE nods, and ATTICUS crosses over to the CHILDREN with CALPURNIA following. The light in the trial area dims. Meanwhile, JEM, SCOUT and DILL are coming over.)*

SCOUT *(to JEM)*. Is he mad?

JEM *(shrugging)*. We'll find out. *(ATTICUS, exhausted, is approaching them, followed by the outraged CALPURNIA.)*

SCOUT *(calling to him as HE comes.)* Hey, Atticus.

JEM *(excitedly)*. We've won, haven't we Atticus?

ATTICUS *(shortly)*. I've no idea. You've been here all afternoon? *(THEY nod.)* Well, go home with Calpurnia and stay home.

JEM. Aw, Atticus. Please let us hear the verdict.

ATTICUS. Have you done your reading today for Mrs. Dubose?

JEM. Not today. *Please*, sir. We—

ATTICUS. Tell you what—you read to Mrs. Dubose, eat your supper, and then Cal can bring you back.

CALPURNIA *(protesting)*. Sir?

ATTICUS. They've heard it all up to now! They might as well hear the rest.

DILL. Suppose the jury comes back before—

ATTICUS. Probably will. They might be out and back in a minute.

JEM. You think they'll acquit him that fast?

ATTICUS *(quietly)*. Go do your reading, eat your supper, and if the jury is still out when you get back, you can wait up there with Cal and hear the verdict. *(Deeply appreciative.)* Thank you, Cal. *(As the light on them is dimming, CALPURNIA starts to herd JEM, SCOUT, and DILL off. ATTICUS watches them go.)*

CALPURNIA *(indignantly, as THEY go)*. I should skin every one of you alive! The very idea—you children listening to all that! Mister Jem, don't you know better 'n to take your little sister to that trial? As for you, Mister Dill, you watch out your aunt doesn't ship you back to Meridian first thing in the mornin'! You oughta be perfectly ashamed of yourselves. *(THEY exit.)*

*(As ATTICUS turns to walk back into the trial area, HE's suddenly blocked by BOB EWELL. MISS MAUDIE has risen from among the SPECTATORS and SHE sees this.)*

BOB EWELL *(speaking with hushed hatred)*. Finch—better lissen. I'm gonna kill ya—if it takes the rest of my life, ya hear? I'm gonna kill ya! *(The lack of response from ATTICUS infuriates him even more. Contorting with rage, HE spits in ATTICUS' face. MISS MAUDIE gasps. ATTICUS stares at EWELL, then reaches into his pocket. EWELL steps back at this, but what ATTICUS takes out is a handkerchief and starts wiping his face. EWELL, now triumphant, swaggers off. MISS MAUDIE comes into the light with ATTICUS.)*

MISS MAUDIE *(quietly)*. I saw that. *(Quietly furious.)* I think I should speak to Heck Tate.

ATTICUS. Let's not bother Heck.

MISS MAUDIE *(concerned)*. Aren't you going to say anything?

ATTICUS *(with slight nod)*. I wish Bob Ewell would not chew tobacco. *(And HE walks off through the trial area. MISS MAUDIE needs a moment to deal with this.)*

MISS MAUDIE *(unhappily, front)*. At least the children didn't see that. *(Noticing their approach.)* When they came back a few hours later, Calpurnia was still expressing her outrage.

*(As CALPURNIA and the CHILDREN come on.)*

CALPURNIA. Thought you was gettin' some kinda head on your shoulders, Mister Jem. Ain't you got any sense at all?

JEM. Don't *you* want to see what happens?

CALPURNIA *(an angry whisper as THEY go to their seats)*. Hush your mouth, sir. If Mr. Finch don't wear you out, I will!

DILL *(looking out front with glad surprise)*. The jury's still out!

JEM *(looking about as HE sits)*. Nobody's moved hardly.

*(The light on the trial area should not come up yet, but it will be at least partially visible from the spill of light illuminating the SPECTATORS. JUDGE TAYLOR is sitting where HE was, his head on his hand, half asleep. MR. GILMER sits at his table going over some notes. MAYELLA still sits on her bench, but BOB EWELL is not there. ATTICUS is also off, as are HECK TATE and TOM ROBINSON. The SPECTATORS are all in place.)*

REVEREND SYKES *(meanwhile; to JEM)*. They moved around some when the jury went out.

JEM. How long have they been out?

REVEREND SYKES. Hours. Mr. Finch and Mr. Gilmer did some more talkin' and Judge Taylor charged the jury. Seemed like he was mighty fair-minded. Thought he was leanin' a little to our side. Made Mr. Ewell so mad, he stamped out of the room.

JEM. The judge isn't supposed to lean either way. 'Sides, we don't need it 'cause we won anyway.

REVEREND SYKES *(interrupting)*. Mister Jem, I've never seen *any* jury decide in favor of a black man.

JEM. This case is different.

*(At this, BOB EWELL, very full of himself at this moment, crosses to sit with MAYELLA. The trial area, however, is only partially lighted.)*

SCOUT *(concerned)*. Wonder where's Atticus.

DILL *(uneasy)*. That Bob Ewell looks mighty pleased 'bout somethin'.

SCOUT. Jem—ain't it a long time?

JEM *(pleased)*. Sure is, Scout. That could be a good sign.

*(At this point, ATTICUS comes on, crosses to his table and sits.)*

SCOUT *(catches her breath)*. I think something's happening!

DILL *(also breathless)*. Here we go...

*(HECK TATE has come on, and he pauses there, his voice ringing with authority. Light is coming up fully now on the trial area.)*

HECK. This court will come to order.

*(HECK steps back off again. JUDGE TAYLOR is rousing himself to sudden alertness, as is EVERYONE else. HECK reappears quickly, escorting TOM ROBINSON to the table where ATTICUS waits.)*

REVEREND SYKES. Brother Tom—*(TOM looks at him, then turns away quickly to sit beside ATTICUS.)*

JEM *(looks out front with growing dismay).* Scout—Look. Look at the jury comin' in! *(JEM's voice is making DILL nervous; HE is also looking out.)*

DILL. What about 'em?

SCOUT *(as SHE realizes; hushed).* They're *not* looking at the defendant!

DILL *(more nervous).* What does it mean?

HECK *(calling).* The defendant will rise. *(As TOM and ATTICUS are rising, HECK comes down to the front of the stage for an instant, turns and goes back to hand a slip of paper to JUDGE TAYLOR.)*

DILL *(as this is happening; a frantic whisper).* What's it mean, Scout?

SCOUT *(miserable).* You're gonna see.

DILL. See what?

JEM. Hush.

*(JUDGE TAYLOR has read the slip of paper. HE suddenly seems very tired. HE picks up his gavel, ready to*

*rap with it, but sees it is not necessary. HE leans forward.)*

JUDGE TAYLOR. The jury finds the defendant—guilty.

*(There is a sigh from SOME, and intake of breath from OTHERS, and a low moan from CALPURNIA. The JUDGE is about to rap with his gavel, but decides against it again. Wearily, HE tosses the gavel onto the table, leans back and nods to HECK. ATTICUS has put a hand on TOM's shoulder and is speaking earnestly into his ear as HECK TATE approaches. ATTICUS then steps aside and HECK escorts TOM off. BOB EWELL, muttering disdainfully past the JUDGE, goes off, followed by MAYELLA. MR. GILMER also goes off, as does JUDGE TAYLOR. The reactions below are expressed during this and follow as quickly as the verdict registers.)*

SCOUT *(in shock).* We lost! It's all lost!

JEM *(heartbroken).* How could they find him guilty?

CALPURNIA *(an unhappy protest voiced mainly to herself.)* Not right you children should see such things! Not right *any* children should see such things!

DILL *(hushed).* What happens now? What can we do?

JEM *(bitterly).* If the evidence don't matter, I don't see there's anything—

DILL *(whispered horror).* But they're not going to hurt Tom Robinson? Your father'll do something. Mr. Finch won't let 'em. He'll—he—*(DILL is stopped by REVEREND SYKES' hand on his shoulder, and as he looks back, he sees that the REVEREND and CALPURNIA are standing respectfully. He realizes, and rises to his feet as does JEM. Meanwhile ATTICUS has been left alone in the trial area. He has put some papers in his briefcase, and, utterly exhausted, he is collecting himself, unaware of the OTHERS.)*

SCOUT *(her fists clenched, and leaning forward).* They c'n shout mean, hateful things at him and find Tom Robinson guilty! But no matter what any of 'em says—Atticus—he's—

REVEREND SYKES *(his hand on her shoulder now).* Miss Jean Louise—Scout—*(Interrupted, SCOUT turns to see them standing. MISS MAUDIE is also standing to show her respect. The SPECTATORS who have started moving off, carrying their chairs, pause now, possibly out of curiosity, but THEY are also standing.)* Stand up. Stand up—your father's passing. *(SCOUT gets to her feet with the OTHERS as ATTICUS starts across. As this is happening, the lights dim on the trial area, which is cleared away.)*

JEM *(calls).* Atticus—wait! *(ATTICUS stops at the call, looking for them. JEM, DILL, and SCOUT scramble over to where HE is . JEM is close to tears. Speaking with difficulty.)* Atticus—how could the jury—how could they do it?

ATTICUS *(bitter)* I don't know how, but they did it. They've done it before, and they did it today, and they'll do it again. *(Starts off, then stops.)* And when they do it—seems like only children weep. *(Going.)* See you at home.

*(MISS STEPHANIE is coming toward them.)*

DILL *(too much to bear).* We can still do something. Can't we? Something?

JEM *(bitterly)*. Looks to me like the minute Mayella Ewell opened her mouth and screamed, Tom Robinson was a dead man!

DILL *(shocked protest)*. Jem!

MISS STEPHANIE *(busting over)*. I'm absolutely surprised at you children. Did Atticus give you permission to go to court? *(JEM shrugs in reply. MISS MAUDIE is also crossing.)* Why were you sitting over in the colored balcony? Several people mentioned it. Wasn't it right close over there?

MISS MAUDIE *(disgusted)*. Hush, Stephanie.

MISS STEPHANIE *(turning)*. Do *you* think it's wise for children to—

MISS MAUDIE *(interrupting)*. We've made the town this way for them. They might as well learn to cope with it.

MISS STEPHANIE. Least they don't have to wallow in it.

MISS MAUDIE *(tartly)*. What happened in court is as much a part of Maycomb as missionary teas.

MISS STEPHANIE *(going)*. Well—excuse me. Don't suppose they understood anyway. *(MISS STEPHANIE pauses before going, and speaks with what may be genuine sympathy.)* Too bad you had to see your daddy get beat. *(With this, MISS STEPHANIE goes in. JEM and SCOUT are hurt by her comment, as is DILL.)*

DILL *(beginning softly)*. When I get grown, I think I'll be a clown.

JEM *(not quite focusing)*. What, Dill?

DILL. Yes, sir, a clown. There ain't one thing in this world I can *do* about folks, so I'm gonna join the circus and laugh my head off.

JEM. You've got it backwards, Dill. Clowns are sad. It's folks that laugh at them.

DILL. I'm gonna be a new kind of clown. I'm gonna stand in the middle of the ring and laugh—laugh in their faces!

*(MISS MAUDIE has been watching, disturbed by their unhappiness.)*

MISS MAUDIE. Don't pay attention to what *she* says about Atticus.

JEM. What do you mean?

MISS MAUDIE. I simply would like you to know that there are some men in this world who were born to do our unpleasant jobs for us. Your father's one of them.

JEM. Oh—well—

MISS MAUDIE. Don't you 'oh well' me, sir. You're just not old enough to appreciate what I said.

JEM *(troubled)*. I always thought Maycomb folks were the best folks in the world.

MISS MAUDIE. We're the safest folks in the world. We're so rarely called on to be Christians, but when we are, we've got men like Atticus to go for us.

JEM. Who feels that way 'sides you?

MISS MAUDIE. The handful of people in this town who say that fair play isn't marked 'White Only.'

JEM *(must know)*. But who? Who did one thing to help Tom Robinson?

MISS MAUDIE. His friends, for one thing, and people like us. We exist, too. People like Judge Taylor. People like Heck Tate. Start using your head, Jem. Did it ever strike you that Judge Taylor naming Atticus to defend Tom was no accident? That Judge Taylor might have had his reasons?

SCOUT. S'right, Jem. Usually the court appoints some new lawyer—one who is just startin'.

MISS MAUDIE. You're beginning to realize! A little more to it than you thought! *(Pressing.)* Whether Maycomb knows it or not, we're paying your father the highest tribute we can pay a man. We trust him to do right.

SCOUT. Then why did he get beat?

MISS MAUDIE *(snorting)*. Miss Stephanie talks nonsense. Maybe he didn't get an acquittal, but he got something. I was sitting in court waiting, and as I waited, I thought —Atticus Finch won't win, he can't win, but he's the only man in these parts who can keep a jury out so long in a case like this. And I thought to myself, maybe we're taking a little step...a little step along the way. *(JEM, SCOUT, and DILL are looking at MISS MAUDIE and thinking about what SHE has just said. SHE takes a breath and collects herself.)* I'm going to my kitchen now, and I'm going to make a cake. And I'd be pleased if you'd all come over later and have some of my cake.

SCOUT *(subdued)*. Yes, Miss Maudie.

JEM. Thank you.

MISS MAUDIE. Mister Dill?

DILL *(half jumping)*. Yes—I'll come. Thank you. *(With this, MISS MAUDIE goes onto her porch. SHE turns to look back at the CHILDREN.)* I better stop over to Aunt Rachel. *(Pauses. Considering.)* They trust him to do right. *(But this is too much for right now. HE'll think about it some other time. Suddenly brightening.)* I'll be back—and then we'll all have cake. *(With this, DILL runs off. SCOUT takes JEM's hand and THEY go into the house.)*

MISS MAUDIE *(from porch, front)*. Tom Robinson was taken to the Enfield Prison Farm, about seventy miles away. Atticus thought Tom had a good chance for a new trial, but Tom just couldn't hope anymore. His old employer made a job for Helen so she could support the children, but she had to pass the Ewell place and they shouted and chucked things at her. She was terrified till Heck Tate went out and made them desist. When Ewell walked out of the courtroom, he expected to find himself the town hero, but it turned out nobody really believed him. All Ewell got for his pain was, 'Okay, we convicted the Negro, but now you get back to your dump.' Bob Ewell's threats got worse, but Atticus just went about his business—working on Tom's appeal. Then suddenly death was among us.

*(JEM, in shock, is coming out of MRS. DUBOSE's house, and stepping down into the yard.)*

MISS MAUDIE. First it was Mrs. Dubose. When Jem was reading to her, he saw she was in trouble. He called his father—but it was too late.

*(ATTICUS comes out of MRS. DUBOSE's house and starts down to JEM.)*

MISS MAUDIE. Her pain was over. *(She goes inside.)*
JEM *(as ATTICUS comes up to him)*. That's why I had to read to her?
ATTICUS *(nods)*. She'd been given morphine for her pain, and she'd become an addict. She wanted to break herself of it before she died. Your reading to her was a distraction.
JEM. I never knew...

*(BOB EWELL, whittling a piece of wood with a knife, is coming slowly onstage. He is full of a private joke that gives him a momentary sense of superiority.)*

ATTICUS *(nodding)*. Her view on a lot of things were quite different from mine, but I was glad she asked you to read to her because I wanted you to see—

BOB EWELL *(cutting in)*. Hello, Finch. *(ATTICUS looks at him, then turns back to JEM.)*

ATTICUS *(continuing)*. I wanted you to see what *real* courage is.

BOB EWELL *(gloating)*. Got some good news, Finch.

ATTICUS *(glancing at EWELL)* Courage isn't a man with a knife in his hand. Jem—it's when you know you're licked before you begin, but you begin anyway and you see it through no matter what. You rarely win—but *sometimes* you do. Mrs. Dubose won, all ninety-eight pounds of her! She died clean as the mountain air!

BOB EWELL. Don't'cha wanta hear, Finch?

*(HECK TATE is coming onstage quickly and CAL-PURNIA and SCOUT are coming out of the house.)*

HECK *(calling)*. Atticus—

ATTICUS. What is it?

HECK. Got news... *(CALPURNIA puts an arm around SCOUT.)*

ATTICUS *(to HECK)*. Tell me.

BOB EWELL *(getting back at them)*. I'll tell you—they shot that nigger!

HECK *(ignoring EWELL)*. Tom's dead!

SCOUT. They shot Tom!

ATTICUS. Heck?

HECK *(nodding)*. He was running. It was during the exercise period. They said he just broke into a blind raving charge at the fence and started climbing over—right in front of them.

ATTICUS. Oh, my God! *(Turning to CALPURNIA.)* Cal, take the children inside.

BOB EWELL. They put seventeen bullet holes in him.

ATTICUS *(to his numb CHILDREN)*. I said for you to go inside. *(ATTICUS turns to HECK; HE does not see that the CHILDREN are not moving.)* Didn't they try to stop him? Didn't they give him any warning?

HECK *(nodding)*. They shouted, and then they fired a few shots into the air. They didn't shoot at him till he was almost over the fence.

SCOUT. How could they shoot *Tom*?

ATTICUS *(with difficulty)*. To them he was just an escaping prisoner. He wasn't *Tom* to them.

JEM *(bewildered)*. Why didn't he wait for the appeal?

ATTICUS. I told him we had a chance, but I guess Tom was fed up with white men's chances.

BOB EWELL. Ain't it just like a nigger to cut 'n' run?

CALPURNIA *(firmly)* You come inside, Scout.

*(ATTICUS turns to address BOB EWELL directly; HE is barely able to control his anger.)*

ATTICUS. Do you have anything more you want to say, Mr. Ewell?

BOB EWELL *(starts to go, then stops overwhelmed with spite)*. Yes—I say there's one down—*(With his knife, EWELL slashes a piece from his whittling.)*—two to go! Now guess who's gonna be next! *(BOB EWELL slashes another piece from his whittling and walks offstage.)*

HECK *(thoughtfully)*. I think I'd keep a shotgun loaded with double O.

JEM *(from the porch)* He doesn't have a shotgun.

ATTICUS. I can't believe Bob Ewell would ever really come after me. But if he should, I'll deal with him.

HECK *(considering)*. I expect you would.

ATTICUS *(dropping his voice)*. Was Tom shot seventeen times?

HECK *(unhappily)*. There's talk, but I don't know. You better be careful, Atticus.

ATTICUS *(after him)*. Sure—thanks, Heck.

JEM *(firmly)*. Atticus, I'm worried about you. And I think you should get a gun.

ATTICUS. I told you twice to go inside. *(They start to go in. Pointedly.)* And remember—we've heard enough about guns.

*(As ATTICUS and JEM go into the house, the light begins to dim except for an isolated light on MISS MAUDIE.)*

MISS MAUDIE. I had a talk with Atticus, but he insisted things would settle down again—after a fashion, he said. And they did. The Maycomb ladies arranged a pageant at the school auditorium with taffy pulls, apple bobbing, and children costumed to represent the county's agricultural products—a girl butterbean, a cow, a peanut—when I saw Jem leave with Scout, she was representing pork—*(Smiles.)* with Jem holding onto her hock. *(Wind is coming up and she looks at sky.)* The clouds were already getting heavy when they left. Looked like it might be storming before they got home. The pageant ended with everyone singing "Maycomb County we will aye be true to thee." Then the children got out of their paper costumes to go home—and Jem and Scout began their longest journey together. *(Wind sounds rising.)* The moon had been in and out of the heavy rainclouds, but as they started home it was black dark—and there was a stillness that comes before a thunderstorm. *(She suddenly shudders, and there's a soft gasp. Half whispers as the light dims out on her.)* Somebody just walked over my grave.

*(There's a flash of lightning and a rumble of thunder. In the flash we see JEM and SCOUT, just on stage.)*

JEM *(sharply)*. Stop! I think I hear something.

SCOUT *(hushed)*. You tryin' to scare me?

JEM. C'mon! *(There are sounds of several steps being taken, then they stop. Fear in his voice.)* Someone's following us! *(Thunder. The stage is dark.)* Keep hold of my hand.

SCOUT. Jem, are you afraid?

JEM. Think we're almost home.

SCOUT. Reckon we ought to sing, Jem?

JEM *(worried)*. No. Be real quiet, Scout. Listen. *(There is the sound of SOMEONE running toward them.)*

SCOUT *(with sudden alarm)*. I hear! Jem!

JEM *(shouting imperatively)*. He's coming! Run, Scout! Run! Run!

SCOUT *(in trouble)*. I tripped! Jem—help me!

JEM *(frantic)*. Where are ya? Scout—C'mon!

SCOUT *(growing panic)*. Can't see! I don't know where—

JEM. Get away, Scout—*Run!* *(Then JEM cries out as SOMEONE grabs him. There is a sound of struggling A MAN's VOICE is heard—angry, unintelligible.)*

ATTACKER. Got'cha—now you'll—damn ya-show
  'em—*(There is a crack and JEM screams with pain.)*
SCOUT *(hushed terror)*. Jem! *(A cry.)* Help us—someone
  —help!

*(The blackness is split as the Radley door is suddenly
swung wide open, the light from inside silhouetting a
BIG MAN in the doorway. There may be a clap of thunder accompanying this action. The light may briefly re-
veal an ATTACKER standing over JEM on the ground,
and struggling with the stricken SCOUT. The less seen
the better. The light is quickly cut off as the BIG MAN
slams the door behind him and joins the struggle in the
darkness. There is a moment of continued struggle,
grunts, SCOUT's sobs, and then the ATTACKER's cry
of pain: 'Ahhhh!' The sounds of a struggle stop. JEM is
picked up by the BIG MAN from the Radley house and
carried to the Finch house, where the porch light is
turned on, and ATTICUS comes out. JEM's arm is hanging as though broken. SCOUT, who has been flung to
the ground, is watching from there. The ATTACKER is
not visible. ATTICUS is coming out.)*

ATTICUS. Who called? What is it? Who—*(Stopping him-
self as he sees the BIG MAN approaching with JEM.
ATTICUS goes off the porch to help him.)* Oh, my God
—Jem! *(ATTICUS helps the BIG MAN with JEM. Call-
ing ahead.)* Cal—telephone Doctor Reynolds quick!
Tell him *urgent!* *(The BIG MAN is taking JEM inside.)*
Put him down on—*(Turning.)* Scout—where's Scout?
SCOUT *(struggling up)*. I'm here! *(ATTICUS rushes to
her.)* I'm all right—the man's gone. But he did some-
thing to Jem. Atticus—is Jem dead?

ATTICUS (*taking her back to the porch*). He's unconscious. Looks like his arm's broken.

(*CALPURNIA is coming out onto the porch.*)

CALPURNIA. Scout all right?
ATTICUS. Yes.
CALPURNIA. Miss Eula May's getting Doctor Reynolds.
SCOUT (*needing reassurance*). Jem's not dead, is he, Cal?
CALPURNIA. Passed out from the pain. Who did this? Who would—
ATTICUS. Call Heck Tate. Tell him someone's been after my children.

(*CALPURNIA gives a hard stare into the night and goes inside. SCOUT, numb, sits quietly on the swing. ATTICUS, unaware of SCOUT, experiences an explosion of anger he can't entirely control. He wants to pound walls, break furniture. He fights for control, but a cry of rage bursts out of him. Then he takes several breaths, gets hold of himself, and goes into the house.*)

MISS MAUDIE (*takes a deep breath, trying to deal with her own strong emotions. Her voice is tight*). After ten forevers, Doctor Reynolds finished with Jem. Said it looked like someone tried to wring his arm off. Said it would be a while before he could play football again. Told Scout Jem positively was not dead.

(*HECK TATE, with flashlight, has come onstage and is approaching the porch.*)

HECK (*calling*). Atticus—

*(ATTICUS comes onto the porch.)*

ATTICUS. Come in, Heck. Did you find anything? *(Incredulous.)* I can't conceive anyone who'd do this.

HECK. Let's stay outside. *(SCOUT is watching from the porch as ATTICUS steps down to HECK.)*

ATTICUS *(puzzled)*. What is it?

HECK. Bob Ewell's lyin' on the ground yonder with a kitchen knife stuck up under his ribs. He's dead, Mr. Finch.

*(ATTICUS is stunned, and SCOUT gulps. The BIG MAN comes out of the house, standing quietly, watching from back by the porch swing.)*

ATTICUS *(bleakly)*. Dead? Are you sure?

HECK. Good and dead. He won't hurt these children again.

ATTICUS. But—

HECK *(his anger getting the better of him)*. The mean-as-hell, low-down skunk with enough liquor in him to make him brave enough to kill children!

ATTICUS *(in shock)*. I thought he'd got it out of him the day he spat at me. And if he hadn't, I thought *I* was the one he'd come after.

HECK. Now you know better. *(To SCOUT.)* He broke Jem's arm, and he grabbed you. Then what happened?

SCOUT. Someone came out—to help. Someone—

HECK. Who was it?

SCOUT *(becoming aware of him)*. Well, there he is, Mr. Tate—he'll tell you his name. *(They ALL turn to look at the BIG MAN at the back of the porch. HE is pale, nervous, withdrawn. As SCOUT looks at him, SHE be-*

*gins to realize; SHE takes a step toward him. Gently.)*
Hey—Boo.

ATTICUS *(to SCOUT).* His right name's Mr. Arthur—Boo
is just a nickname. Jean Louise, this is Mr. Arthur Radley. Maybe you'd like to take him in. You can sit by
Jem.

SCOUT. Like to come in, Mr. Boo? *(HE nods. SHE takes
his hand and leads him in.)*

ATTICUS *(turning).* Well, Heck—I guess the thing to do
—Jem's a minor, of course. It'll come before county
court.

HECK. What will, Mr. Finch?

ATTICUS. Of course it's clear-cut self-defense.

HECK. Mr. Finch, do you think Jem killed Bob Ewell?

ATTICUS. They were struggling in the dark. He probably
got hold of Ewell's knife.

HECK. It wasn't Jem.

ATTICUS. That's kind of you, and I know you're doing it
from the good of your heart. But I won't have him grow
up with a whisper about him. I won't hush up—

HECK *(sharply)* Hush up what? Jem didn't do it.

ATTICUS. Then who—

HECK *(flatly).* I'll tell you—Bob Ewell fell on his knife.
He killed himself.

ATTICUS. Heck, I won't have my children hear me say
something different from what they know to be true. If
I do, I won't have them anymore. I can't live one way
in town and another way in my home.

HECK. Mr. Finch, I hate to fight you when you're like
this. You've been under a strain no man should ever
have to go through. Maybe that's why you're not putting two and two together.

ATTICUS *(trying to understand).* If it wasn't Jem—

HECK. Of course it wasn't. His arm was broken.

ATTICUS *(looking toward the porch)*. Then it was—it would have to be—

HECK *(emphatically)*. Put that thought outa your mind, Mr. Finch. I already told you what happened.

*(SCOUT is coming back onto the porch.)*

ATTICUS. But if it was—

HECK. This isn't your decision, Mr. Finch, it's all mine. It's my decision, and my responsibility. And there's not much you can do about it.

ATTICUS. What are you saying, Heck?

HECK. I'm saying there's a black man dead for no reason, and the white man responsible for it is dead. So let the dead bury the dead, this time, Mr. Finch.

ATTICUS. What about—

HECK. I never heard tell it's against the law for a citizen to do his utmost to prevent a crime from being committed, which is exactly what Boo Radley did. Now maybe you'll say it's my duty to tell the town all about it and not hush it up. Know what'd happen then? All the ladies in Maycomb, including my wife, would be knocking on the door bringing angel food cakes. To my way of thinking, dragging him with his shy ways into the limelight—that's a sin. *(HECK starts to go, then pauses.)* I may not be much, Mr. Finch, but I'm still sheriff of Maycomb County, and Bob Ewell fell on his knife. *(Going.)* Good night, sir. *(ATTICUS turns and is surprised to see SCOUT.)*

ATTICUS. Scout.

SCOUT. Yes, Atticus?

ATTICUS. Mr. Ewell fell on his knife. Can you possibly understand?

SCOUT. Sir—it looks to me—what Heck said—

*(SCOUT is interrupted by BOO, who has come back onto the porch.)*

BOO. Jean Louise?

SCOUT. Yes, Mr. Boo?

BOO. Will you take me home?

SCOUT *(nods)*. Mr. Arthur, bend your arm down here, like that. That's right, sir. *(SHE slips her hand into the crook of his arm.)*

ATTICUS *(after them)*. Arthur—*(SCOUT and BOO pause.)* Thank you for my children. *(Then SCOUT and BOO continue toward the Radley house.)*

MISS MAUDIE *(as THEY walk, front)*. The moon had come out—the storm had passed over—and I couldn't help hoping Miss Stephanie was watching from her upstairs window, seeing *Arthur Radley* escorting Miss Jean Louise as any gentleman would do. *(THEY go up onto the Radley porch. BOO gently releases his arm and goes inside. SCOUT stands for a moment on the porch.)* None of us ever saw him again. But—I saw something else. Neighbors bring food with death, and flowers with sickness, and Boo was our neighbor. He gave two children a pair of slicked-up good luck pennies, a stick of chewing gum, and their lives. *(Calling to SCOUT who is coming back from the porch, half in a trance.)* Miss Jean Louise?

SCOUT. Didn't have to stand in Boo Radley's shoes to know him. Just standing on his porch was enough.

MISS MAUDIE *(concerned)*. You feel all right, girl?

SCOUT *(it's strange)*. I feel old. Jem and I still have to get grown, but there isn't much else left for us to learn —except possibly algebra.

MISS MAUDIE *(smiling. Going)*. Expect you'll handle it.

SCOUT *(sees ATTICUS. Runs up onto porch)*. Is Jem awake yet?

ATTICUS. Sleeping peacefully. Won't be awake till morning.

SCOUT. Atticus—what Heck Tate said about Boo—about dragging him into the limelight—Heck was right.

ATTICUS. What do you mean?

SCOUT. I mean, it'd be sort of like shooting a mockingbird, wouldn't it?

ATTICUS *(nods, smiling)*. Let's go in and sit with Jem.

SCOUT *(as THEY are going)*. All those ideas we had about Boo Radley—But, Atticus—he's *real* nice. *(The curtain, if used, is falling. Otherwise the lights are dimming.)*

ATTICUS *(affectionately)*. Most people are, Scout—when you finally see them. *(THEY are going inside as the lights dim to black.)*

## THE END

# PRODUCTION NOTES

## SETTING

There may be a curtain, but it isn't necessary. The set which stands throughout the play can be visible to the audience as they take their seats in the theatre.

The intention of the set is to suggest a part of a house and the immediate neighborhood just outside, in a small town in the southern part of Alabama. It is 1935, and while the set need not reflect this in detail, a few props that suggest the period (available, no doubt, from someone's attic) are recommended.

The stage has two levels. At the right on the lower level is the porch of the Finch home. It has several old rockers, chairs, possibly an old-fashioned radio and a porch swing or glider.

On the upper level, suggesting the street, are several narrow porch fronts with doorways behind. The porches have railings, and if desired, there may be flowers or shrubs about them. The Dubose porch, ULC, should have at least a few potted flowers. The actors must have access to these porches from behind, and there should be a passageway in front of the porches, but still on the platform, on which an actor can cross the stage from right to left. This passageway also makes room for an inner curtain that can be drawn across (or lowered) in front of the upper level porches.

At the left side of the stage is a part of another house. It's a slate-gray house with dark green shutters beside a window with heavy curtains behind. There is a closed door and a picket fence. The place is neglected, and to a child, it could seem ominous. It is on the upper level, though the little section of picket fence is in front of it on the lower level. Just outside the fence and at the left is a tree.

Actors bring in chairs and a few props when the scene becomes the courthouse.

## NOTES ABOUT CHARACTERS

GENERAL NOTE ABOUT ALL CHARACTERS.

Everyone in this play lives in southern Alabama and accordingly might be expected to speak with a Southern accent. It would be a disservice to the play, however, if the audience starts admiring the accent rather than listening to the content of the lines. The playwright strongly urges that the actors understate any attempt at a regional accent rather than risk overstating it—thus calling attention to it and hurting the flow of the play. An authentic pattern of Southern speech is already contained in the lines, and this is sufficient.

SCOUT: A young girl about to experience the events that will shape the rest of her life, she should, ideally, seem as young as nine. Scout is courageous and forthright. If a question occurs to her, she'll ask it.

JEM: He is a few years older than his sister Scout, and like his sister—perhaps even more than his sister—he's reaching out to understand their unusual and thus not conventionally-admirable father. Probably the strongest undercurrent in Jem is his desire to communicate with his father.

ATTICUS: He's tall, quietly impressive, reserved, civilized and nearly fifty. He wears glasses and because of the poor sight in his left eye, looks with his right eye when he wants to see something well. It's typical of Atticus that when he found out he was an extraordinary shot with a rifle, he gave up shooting—because he considered it gave him an unfair advantage over the animals. He's quietly courageous and without heroics, he does what he considers just. As someone comments about him—'We trust him to do right.'

CALPURNIA: Black, proud and capable, she has raised the motherless Scout and Jem. She's a self-educated woman and she's made quite a good job of it. Her standards are high and her discipline as applied to Scout and Jem is uncompromising.

DILL: Small, blond and wise beyond his years, he is about the same age as Jem. Dill is neater and better dressed than his friends. There's an undercurrent of sophistication to him, but his laugh is sudden and happy. Obviously there is a lack in his own home life, and he senses something in Atticus that's missing from his own family relationship.

MAUDIE ATKINSON: Younger than Atticus, but of his generation, she's a lovely sensitive woman. Though belonging to the time and place of this play, she has a wisdom and compassion that suggests the best instincts of the South of that period.

WALTER CUNNINGHAM: Cunningham is a hard-up farmer who shares the prejudices of this time and place but who is nevertheless a man who can be reached as a human being. He also has seeds of leadership, for when his attitude is changed during the confrontation with Atticus, he takes the others with him.

REVEREND SYKES: Rev. Sykes is the black minister of the First Purchase Church, called that because it was paid for with the first money earned by the freed slaves. He's an imposing man with a strong stage presence. He should have a strong "minister's" voice.

HECK TATE: Heck is the town sheriff and a complex man. He does his duty as he sees it, and enforces the law without favor. The key to this man's actual feelings is revealed in his final speeches to Atticus, and this attitude should be an undercurrent to his earlier actions.

STEPHANIE CRAWFORD: She's a neighborhood gossip, and she enjoys it to the hilt. There's an enthusiasm in her talking over the people of her town that makes it almost humorous. Sometime she says things that are petty, but partly it's because she simply can't keep herself from stirring things up.

BOO RADLEY: Arthur Radley is a pale recluse who hasn't been outside his house in fifteen years. It takes an extraordinary emergency to bring him out, and once out he's uncertain about how to deal with people, and with his mission accomplished, he's eager to return to his sanctuary.

MRS. DUBOSE: She is an old woman—ill, walking with difficulty, her pain making her biting, bitter, and angry. However, she's fighting a secret battle within herself, a battle about which few people are aware, and her existence has in it a point of importance for Jem and Scout.

TOM ROBINSON: Robinson is black, handsome and vital, but with a left hand crippled by a childhood accident and held against his chest. He's married to Helen and they have young children. He faces up to a false charge with quiet dignity. There's an undercurrent in him of kindness, sensitivity and consideration.

JUDGE TAYLOR: The judge is a wintry man of the South, who does what he can within the context of his time to see justice done in his court. While he tries to run his court impartially, his sympathy is with Tom.

MR. GILMER: He is a public prosecutor who is doing his job in trying to convict Tom. In many ways his manner is cruel and hurtful. And yet under all this, he too has unexpressed doubts as to Tom's guilt, and his heart isn't really in this conviction. Still—he goes after it, and it's a hard thing.

BOB EWELL: Ewell is a little bantam-cock of a man who lives with his large family by the town dump. As Harper Lee describes their situation—'The town gave them Christmas baskets, welfare money, and the back of their hand.' Bob thinks this trial will make him an important man, and when Atticus destroys his credibility, Bob's rage and frustration border on paranoia.

MAYELLA: The oldest daughter of Bob Ewell, she's a desperately lonely and overworked young woman whose need for companionship—any companionship—has overwhelmed every other emotion. However, when her effort to reach out explodes in her face, she fights just as desperately for what she thinks is survival.

## NOTES ON COSTUMES

The time of the play is 1935 and the setting is a small town in a rural area of southern Alabama. The costumes should *suggest* this time and place; while there is no objection to the costumes being entirely authentic, this certainly isn't necessary. It should be remembered that this was the time of the great depression and there was very little money in towns like Maycomb, Alabama.

The professional men such as Atticus, Judge Taylor and Mr. Gilmer wear business clothes, but they're old business clothes. Heck Tate wears a combination of business-work clothes. Such ladies as Maudie Atkinson and Stephanie Crawford wear quite nice clothes, but probably they've been kept nice by careful repair. Tom Robinson and Walter Cunningham wear neat, clean farm clothes — but they should obviously be worn and used. Calpurnia dresses in impeccably neat work clothes, because that's the way she is. Mrs. Dubose is ill and even though she lives in a warm climate, she wants to be warmer, and she should have an old shawl. Mayella and her father wear clothes that have been given to them — not absurd misfits, but at least suggesting that they're second-hand. Reverend Sykes wears a conservative dark suit, white shirt, and dark tie. Scout and Jem wear sensible play clothes — at the beginning Scout wears bib-overalls. Dill is better dressed and more conscious of his appearance than the others. Boo Radley, being a recluse, wears shabby comfortable clothes.

## PROPERTIES

## GENERAL

Street: Porch fronts with railings, practical doors behind them; picket fence; tree; rockers, chairs, old-fashioned radio, porch swing on Finch porch; potted flowers, chair draped with shawls on Dubose porch; shutters and curtains at window of Radley house; flowers or shrubs about houses (optional).

Courtroom: Judge's bench and chair, witness chair, small table and chair, table with two chairs.

## PERSONAL

SCOUT: Piece of gum and small box (supposedly taken from knothole in tree).

CALPURNIA: Dish cloth.

HECK TATE: Heavy rifle; slip of paper, flashlight.

JUDGE TAYLOR: Gavel.

MRS. DUBOSE: Cane.

JEM: Football; small flashlight.

ATTICUS: Eyeglasses, briefcase, small folding chair, electrical extension cord with light bulb on end, standing hat rack, newspaper, handkerchief, envelope and fountain pen in pocket, papers.

MR. CUNNINGHAM: Sack.

SPECTATORS at Trial: Small folding chairs.

BOB EWELL: Piece of wood, knife.

MR. GILMER: Papers.

## FROM THE PLAYWRIGHT...

Meeting with Harper Lee to discuss the stage adaptation of her extraordinary book *TO KILL A MOCKINGBIRD* was an event about which I felt some trepidation.

She was born Nellie Harper Lee in 1926 in the small town of Monroeville, Alabama, the youngest of three children born to Amasa Coleman Lee and France Finch Lee. It will not surprise you that her father was a lawyer or that she had a childhood friend named Truman Capote who is often thought to be "Dill."

In 1945 she became a law student at the University of Alabama and later became an exchange student at Oxford University, which she left before graduating to go to New York City and to write. The first manuscript of *TO KILL A MOCKINGBIRD* was submitted for publication in 1957, but was not published until 1960 after a great deal of additional work. It was an immediate success, being selected by the Literary Guild and recommended by the Book of the Month Club. It was the basis of an outstanding Academy Award film starring Gregory Peck in the role of Atticus. Since then the book has sold well over fifteen million copies!

My father, Roger Sergel, who had been Professor of English at the University of Pittsburgh and who had been close to many leading writers of his day—Sherwood Anderson dedicated a book to him—particularly admired Harper Lee's book. He died before I met with Harper Lee, but I can still remember his unqualified enthusiasm for her work. When *TO KILL A MOCKINGBIRD* won the Pulitzer Prize, my father said, "This is the first time I entirely agree with the Pulitzer Prize."

Prior to meeting directly with Harper Lee I had a number of useful discussions with Maurice Crain who was a creative force in her life, as to some extent he was in mine. Lucille Sullivan of that office was also a source of excellent advice on this project.

The meeting with Harper Lee, as I recall it from twenty years ago, took place at the Hotel Pierre in New York City. It began as an early lunch and lasted several hours. As we discussed the adaptation and the reasons for the choices being made, I had a sense that she felt the work was on the right track which, of course, was due at least in part to the good advice I'd been given earlier by Maurice Crain. The good discussion continued with Harper Lee as we walked down the hotel corridor. Passing a row of public phones I had an irrational wish that I could call my father and tell him that I'd met with Harper Lee herself and the meeting had gone very well.

A taxi stopped in front and I opened the door for Harper Lee. She embraced me and was gone. I've never seen her again.

Perhaps the essence of what I believe she does better than any writer I know is captured in a brief response Atticus makes to a question from his daughter Scout. In the book as in the play, Tom Robinson, a black man, is wrongly convicted of a crime he did not commit and is later shot down by prison guards as he tries to escape. In anguish Scout asks her father how such a thing could be done to Tom. Atticus replies, "Because he wasn't 'Tom' to them." The special beauty of Harper Lee's work is that she takes us inside the people of her book, and in their various individual ways, each becomes "Tom" to us.

Christopher Sergel<br>
Playwright